FLORIDA
BEACH LIFE

New Smyrna Beach Real Estate Guide

Michael R. Linton, NCREA, CREIPS
Real Estate Professional
Author

FLORIDA BEACH LIFE
New Smyrna Beach Real Estate Guide

Copyright © 2024 by Michael Linton

All rights reserved. No part of this book may be reproduced, distributed, or transmitted in any form or by any means, including photocopying, recording, or other electronic or mechanical methods, without the prior written permission of the publisher, except in the case of brief quotations embodied in critical reviews and certain other noncommercial uses permitted by copyright law.

ISBN: 9798326741271

Published by Michael Linton

Imprint: Independently published

Cover design by Michael Linton

Interior layout and design by Michael Linton

Printed in the USA

First Edition: May 2024

For permission requests, write to the publisher at michael@lintonglobal.com

Michael R. Linton, Author, Real Estate Broker eXp Realty
www.FloridaBeachLife.com

FLORIDA BEACH LIFE
New Smyrna Beach Real Estate Guide

This book is a work of nonfiction. Names, characters, places, and incidents are the product of the author's actual experience. Any resemblance to actual events, locales, or persons, living or dead, is entirely coincidental.

Visit our website at FloridaBeachLife.com

Manufactured in the USA

Printed on acid-free paper

FLORIDA BEACH LIFE
New Smyrna Beach Real Estate Guide

Dedication

To my Lord and Savior, Jesus Christ,

With deep humility and reverence, I dedicate my life and my work to you. Your unwavering guidance, infinite grace, and profound wisdom have been my steadfast companions on this incredible journey. In every step and through every challenge, Your light has shone brightly, guiding me through. For Your constant and unyielding support, I am eternally grateful.

To my beloved wife and invaluable partner, Peggy Linton,

Your steadfast commitment and insightful wisdom have been the foundation of all my achievements. Your love is a ceaseless wellspring of strength and inspiration. This book stands as a heartfelt homage to the incredible partnership we share, intertwined in the deep bonds of marriage and our collaborative endeavors.

FLORIDA BEACH LIFE
New Smyrna Beach Real Estate Guide

Table of Contents

New Smyrna Beach Real Estate Guide
Dedication
Table of Contents
Introduction To Living In New Smyrna Beach
Legal Disclaimer
Introduction:
Chapter 1: Introduction to New Smyrna Beach
    History and Culture
    Attractions and Activities
    Arts and Culture
    Quality of Life
    Real Estate Overview
Chapter 2: Understanding the Local Real Estate Market
    Market Trends and Statistics
    Economic and Demographic Factors
    Neighborhood Insights
    Investment Opportunities
    Future Outlook
Chapter 3: Finding Your Perfect Home in New Smyrna Beach
    Identifying Your Needs and Preferences
    Starting Your Property Search
    Evaluating Potential Homes
    Making an Offer
    Closing the Deal

Michael R. Linton, Author, Real Estate Broker eXp Realty
www.FloridaBeachLife.com

FLORIDA BEACH LIFE
New Smyrna Beach Real Estate Guide

Chapter 4: Key Neighborhoods and Communities
    Beachside Neighborhoods
    Mainland Neighborhoods
    Historic Districts
    Family-Friendly Neighborhoods
    Luxury Communities
    Active Adult Communities

Chapter 5: Navigating the Home Buying Process
    Preparing to Buy
    Starting Your Property Search
    Making an Offer
    Inspections and Appraisals
    Finalizing Financing
    Closing the Deal

Chapter 6: Financing Your New Home
    Understanding Mortgage Options
    Preparing for the Mortgage Application
    Choosing a Lender
    Managing Your Finances During the Home Buying Process

Chapter 7: Selling Your Property
    Preparing Your Property for Sale
    Setting the Right Price
    Marketing Your Property
    Negotiating Offers
    Closing the Sale

Chapter 8: Marketing Strategies for Sellers

Michael R. Linton, Author, Real Estate Broker eXp Realty
www.FloridaBeachLife.com

FLORIDA BEACH LIFE
New Smyrna Beach Real Estate Guide

    Creating a Marketing Plan
    Professional Photography and Staging
    Digital Marketing Strategies
    Traditional Marketing Strategies
    Leveraging Your Real Estate Agent's Expertise
Chapter 9: Investing in New Smyrna Beach Real Estate
    Understanding the Rental Market
    Evaluating Investment Properties
    Financing Investment Properties
    Managing Your Investment Properties
    Legal and Tax Considerations
    Exit Strategies
Chapter 10: Vacation Rentals and Short-Term Leasing
    Understanding the Vacation Rental Market
    Setting Up Your Vacation Rental
    Marketing Your Vacation Rental
    Managing Bookings and Guest Relations
    Legal and Regulatory Considerations
    Maximizing Rental Income
    Working with Property Management Companies
Chapter 11: Legal Considerations in New Smyrna Beach Real Estate
    Understanding Real Estate Contracts
    Title and Escrow
    Closing Process
    Land Use and Zoning Regulations
    Landlord-Tenant Laws

Michael R. Linton, Author, Real Estate Broker eXp Realty
www.FloridaBeachLife.com

FLORIDA BEACH LIFE
New Smyrna Beach Real Estate Guide

 Working with a Real Estate Attorney
Chapter 12: Working with Real Estate Agents
 Choosing the Right Real Estate Agent
 Communicating Effectively with Your Agent
 Leveraging Your Agent's Resources
 Negotiating the Best Deal
 Supporting You Through Closing
Chapter 13: Home Inspection and Appraisal Insights
 Importance of Home Inspections
 Preparing for a Home Inspection
 Common Issues Found During Inspections
 Understanding Appraisals
 Preparing for an Appraisal
 Navigating Potential Issues
Chapter 14: Closing the Deal: What to Expect
 Understanding the Closing Process
 Preparing for Closing Day
 What Happens on Closing Day
 Post-Closing Steps
Chapter 15: Future Trends and Market Predictions
 Economic Factors Influencing Real Estate
 Demographic Shifts
 Technological Advancements
 Environmental and Sustainability Trends
 Market Predictions for New Smyrna Beach
 Strategies for Success in the Future Market

Michael R. Linton, Author, Real Estate Broker eXp Realty
www.FloridaBeachLife.com

FLORIDA BEACH LIFE
New Smyrna Beach Real Estate Guide

- Final Thoughts
- Buy and Sell Your New Smyrna Beach Property with Michael Linton of eXp Realty
- Introduction
- Why New Smyrna Beach?
  - A Slice of Paradise
  - Thriving Community
- The Buying Process with Michael Linton
  - Step-by-Step Guidance
    - Initial Consultation
    - Home Search
    - Making an Offer
    - Closing the Deal
  - Local Expertise
- Selling Your Home with Michael Linton
  - Preparing Your Home
    - Staging Tips
    - Professional Photography
  - Effective Marketing
  - Negotiating Offers
- FAQs
  - How do I get started with buying or selling my New Smyrna Beach real estate?
  - What makes New Smyrna Beach a great place to live?
  - How can I maximize the value of my home before selling?
  - What kind of support can I expect from Michael Linton during the buying process?

FLORIDA BEACH LIFE
New Smyrna Beach Real Estate Guide

Conclusion

FLORIDA BEACH LIFE
New Smyrna Beach Real Estate Guide

Introduction To Living In New Smyrna Beach

Welcome to "Living in New Smyrna Beach: Florida Beach Life." This book is your ultimate guide to understanding and embracing the unique lifestyle offered by one of Florida's most charming beach towns. Nestled on the Atlantic coast, New Smyrna Beach is a hidden gem known for its laid-back atmosphere, pristine beaches, and vibrant community. Whether you're considering a move to this coastal paradise, planning an extended stay, or simply curious about what makes this town so special, this book will provide you with a detailed and engaging overview of life in New Smyrna Beach.

New Smyrna Beach is not just a place; it's an experience. From its rich history that dates back to the 18th century to its modern-day cultural vibrancy, this town has a lot to offer. It's a place where the past and present blend seamlessly, creating a unique environment that is both welcoming and intriguing. The town's history is etched into its very fabric, with historic sites and buildings standing as testaments to its storied past.

One of the standout features of New Smyrna Beach is, of course, its stunning beaches. With 17 miles of white sandy shores, it's a haven for beach lovers. The beaches here offer something for everyone, whether you're a surfer chasing the

Michael R. Linton, Author, Real Estate Broker eXp Realty
www.FloridaBeachLife.com

FLORIDA BEACH LIFE
New Smyrna Beach Real Estate Guide

perfect wave, a family looking for a relaxing day by the sea, or someone who simply enjoys the tranquility of a coastal sunset. The oceanfront is lined with parks, piers, and recreational areas, making it a hub of activity and a central part of the local lifestyle.

Beyond the beaches, New Smyrna Beach boasts a wealth of outdoor activities and adventures. From kayaking in the Indian River Lagoon to hiking in the nearby state parks, there's no shortage of ways to explore the natural beauty of the area. The town's commitment to preserving its natural environment is evident in the numerous conservation efforts and eco-friendly initiatives in place.

Community is at the heart of life in New Smyrna Beach. The town is home to a diverse and vibrant population, with a strong sense of camaraderie and neighborliness. Local events and festivals are a regular occurrence, providing ample opportunities for residents to come together and celebrate. The local culture is rich with arts, music, and culinary delights, ensuring that there's always something to see, do, and taste.

Real estate in New Smyrna Beach is as varied as the town itself, offering a range of options from beachfront condos to historic homes in charming neighborhoods. Whether you're looking to buy, rent, or invest, the local housing market has something to suit every taste and budget. The town's real estate landscape reflects its unique character, blending modern amenities with historic charm.

Education and schools in New Smyrna Beach are of a high standard, with a range of public and private options available. The local educational institutions are committed to providing quality education, ensuring that families have access to excellent learning opportunities for their children.

Dining and nightlife in New Smyrna Beach are experiences in themselves. The town offers a diverse array of restaurants, cafes, and bars, catering to every palate. From fresh seafood caught locally to international cuisine, there's something to satisfy every craving. The nightlife is vibrant, with live music, beachside bars, and cultural performances that keep the town buzzing after dark.

Arts and entertainment are integral to the local culture. New Smyrna Beach is home to numerous galleries, theaters, and performance spaces, showcasing local talent and attracting artists from around the world. The town's commitment to

FLORIDA BEACH LIFE
New Smyrna Beach Real Estate Guide

the arts is evident in its thriving creative community and the numerous cultural events held throughout the year.

Shopping and supporting local businesses is a way of life in New Smyrna Beach. The town's shops and markets offer a unique blend of local products, artisanal goods, and everyday necessities. The emphasis on local commerce not only supports the economy but also fosters a sense of community and sustainability.

Health and wellness are prioritized in New Smyrna Beach, with numerous facilities and services available to support a healthy lifestyle. From fitness centers and yoga studios to healthcare providers and wellness programs, residents have access to a comprehensive range of health and wellness resources.

Seasonal events and festivals are a highlight of life in New Smyrna Beach. The town's calendar is filled with celebrations that reflect its cultural diversity and community spirit. From beachside concerts and art fairs to food festivals and holiday parades, there's always something to look forward to.

Navigating the local economy is essential for anyone considering a move to New Smyrna Beach. This chapter will provide insights into the economic landscape, employment opportunities, and the business environment, helping you to understand how to thrive in this coastal town.

Retiring in New Smyrna Beach is a dream for many. The town offers a relaxed and fulfilling lifestyle, with plenty of amenities and activities for retirees. Whether you're looking for a quiet place to enjoy your golden years or an active community to stay engaged and social, New Smyrna Beach has it all.

Finally, this book will offer practical tips for new residents, from navigating local services to integrating into the community. Moving to a new place can be challenging, but with the right guidance, it can also be an exciting and rewarding experience.

"Living in New Smyrna Beach: Florida Beach Life" is more than just a guide; it's an invitation to discover and embrace a lifestyle that is as enriching as it is enjoyable. Welcome to your new home in paradise.

Michael R. Linton, Author, Real Estate Broker eXp Realty
www.FloridaBeachLife.com

FLORIDA BEACH LIFE
New Smyrna Beach Real Estate Guide

Legal Disclaimer

As a seasoned commercial broker and real estate investor with 38 years in the industry, I've garnered invaluable insights and experiences that I'm eager to share with you in this book. However, it's vitally important that I commence with a legal disclaimer. While the knowledge and strategies I present are drawn from my long-standing experience, the following pages should not be construed as providing legal, financial, or professional advice.

The realm of real estate investing is intricate and multifaceted. Each property, deal, and situation comes with its unique circumstances. While I've endeavored to deliver precise and up-to-date information, it should be seen as a general guideline or a foundation upon which to build, not as an exhaustive or personalized plan.

Even though I've done my utmost to ensure the information's accuracy at the time of writing, keep in mind that real estate markets are dynamic. Economic conditions, market trends, zoning laws, tax implications, and many other factors influencing a real estate investment can change. Given this fluidity, some details and advice might become less relevant or outdated over time.

Michael R. Linton, Author, Real Estate Broker eXp Realty
www.FloridaBeachLife.com

FLORIDA BEACH LIFE
New Smyrna Beach Real Estate Guide

Moreover, Florida, like all states, has its unique regulations and market specifics. Although many of the principles and strategies I share may have broader applicability, some might be particularly relevant to the Chicagoland market and less so to other locales.

The successes I've enjoyed, which I will share with you, stem from meticulous planning, rigorous research, risk mitigation, and, at times, a little serendipity. Real estate investment involves substantial financial risk, and it is possible to lose part or all of your investment. Therefore, I implore you to seek advice from a certified professional - a lawyer, financial advisor, or real estate professional - before making significant investment decisions.

While this book discusses various investment strategies, their inclusion should not be seen as an endorsement. Each investor must assess their financial situation, risk tolerance, and investment objectives before choosing their course.

Finally, remember that real estate investing, like all worthwhile endeavors, demands dedication, patience, and continuous learning. Success rarely happens overnight; often, it's the product of consistency and resilience amid setbacks.

Michael R. Linton, Author, Real Estate Broker eXp Realty
www.FloridaBeachLife.com

By proceeding with this book, you acknowledge that I - the author, broker, and investor - cannot be held liable for any

decisions you make based on the information provided. You agree to accept all risks linked to real estate investments and understand it is your responsibility to conduct thorough due diligence and consult with professionals as necessary.

With that necessary preamble, I am thrilled to start this journey with you, sharing the strategies, insights, and experiences that have steered my fulfilling career in the vibrant, challenging, yet ultimately rewarding world of real estate investing in Florida.

FLORIDA BEACH LIFE
New Smyrna Beach Real Estate Guide

Introduction:

Welcome to "New Smyrna Beach Real Estate Guide: Florida Beach Life." Whether you are a first-time homebuyer, a seasoned investor, or someone looking to sell your property, this guide is designed to provide you with all the necessary information and insights you need to navigate the New Smyrna Beach real estate market successfully.

New Smyrna Beach, often referred to as NSB, is a charming coastal city located in Volusia County, Florida. Known for its beautiful beaches, vibrant arts scene, and historic charm, New Smyrna Beach has become a sought-after destination for both residents and tourists alike. The city's unique blend of small-town charm and modern amenities makes it an ideal place to live, work, and invest in real estate.

Michael R. Linton, Author, Real Estate Broker eXp Realty
www.FloridaBeachLife.com

FLORIDA BEACH LIFE
New Smyrna Beach Real Estate Guide

In recent years, the real estate market in New Smyrna Beach has experienced significant growth and transformation. With its pristine beaches, favorable climate, and a wide range of recreational activities, it's no wonder that more people are choosing to call this coastal paradise home. However, navigating the real estate market can be a daunting task, especially for those unfamiliar with the area. This guide aims to demystify the process and provide you with a clear roadmap to achieving your real estate goals in New Smyrna Beach.

The first part of this book will introduce you to the city of New Smyrna Beach, providing an overview of its history, culture, and unique attractions. You'll learn about the different neighborhoods and communities that make up the

FLORIDA BEACH LIFE
New Smyrna Beach Real Estate Guide

city, each with its own distinct character and appeal. Understanding the local real estate market is crucial, and we will delve into market trends, property values, and the factors driving demand in the area.

Finding your perfect home in New Smyrna Beach is an exciting journey, and we will guide you through the entire home buying process. From identifying your needs and preferences to viewing properties and making an offer, you'll gain valuable insights and practical tips to ensure a smooth and successful home buying experience. We'll also explore the various financing options available and provide advice on securing the best mortgage for your needs.

Michael R. Linton, Author, Real Estate Broker eXp Realty
www.FloridaBeachLife.com

For those looking to sell their property, this guide offers comprehensive strategies to help you achieve the best possible outcome. From preparing your home for sale and setting the right price to marketing your property and negotiating with buyers, you'll find everything you need to navigate the selling process with confidence. We will also discuss the importance of working with a qualified real estate agent and how to choose the right one for your needs.

Investing in New Smyrna Beach real estate presents a wealth of opportunities, and we will explore the different investment options available. Whether you're interested in long-term rentals, vacation properties, or short-term leasing, you'll gain valuable insights into the local rental market and the potential returns on investment. We'll also cover the legal considerations and regulations you need to be aware of as a property investor in New Smyrna Beach.

The final chapters of this book will provide you with essential information on home inspections, appraisals, and the closing process. You'll learn what to expect during each stage and how to address any potential issues that may arise. We'll also look at future trends and market predictions, giving you a glimpse into what the future holds for the New Smyrna Beach real estate market.

Whether you are a buyer, seller, or investor, "New Smyrna Beach Real Estate Guide" is your ultimate resource for navigating the dynamic and exciting world of New Smyrna Beach real estate. Let's embark on this journey together and

FLORIDA BEACH LIFE
New Smyrna Beach Real Estate Guide

discover the many opportunities that await you in this beautiful coastal city.

FLORIDA BEACH LIFE
New Smyrna Beach Real Estate Guide

Chapter 1: Introduction to New Smyrna Beach

New Smyrna Beach, often referred to as NSB, is a hidden gem on Florida's east coast. With its stunning beaches, vibrant arts community, and rich history, it has become a beloved destination for both tourists and residents. This chapter provides a comprehensive overview of New Smyrna Beach, highlighting its unique characteristics and what makes it such a desirable place to live and invest in real estate.

History and Culture

New Smyrna Beach has a rich history that dates back to its founding in 1768 by Dr. Andrew Turnbull, a Scottish physician and entrepreneur. Turnbull established the colony with settlers from the Mediterranean, creating a diverse and culturally rich community. This heritage is still evident today in the city's architecture, festivals, and cultural events.

The city's history is also deeply intertwined with its natural environment. The Indian River Lagoon, one of the most biologically diverse estuaries in North America, borders New Smyrna Beach, providing a habitat for a wide range of wildlife. The city's commitment to preserving its natural beauty is evident in its numerous parks, nature trails, and conservation efforts.

Attractions and Activities

New Smyrna Beach is renowned for its pristine beaches, which stretch for miles along the Atlantic Ocean. The beach

FLORIDA BEACH LIFE
New Smyrna Beach Real Estate Guide

is a haven for surfers, thanks to its consistently good waves, and it has been named one of the best surf towns in the world. For those who prefer a more relaxed beach experience, the soft, white sands and clear waters provide the perfect setting for sunbathing, swimming, and beachcombing.

In addition to its beaches, New Smyrna Beach offers a wealth of recreational activities. The Indian River Lagoon and the surrounding waters are ideal for boating, fishing, kayaking, and paddleboarding. The city's parks and nature reserves provide ample opportunities for hiking, birdwatching, and wildlife viewing.

Arts and Culture

FLORIDA BEACH LIFE
New Smyrna Beach Real Estate Guide

New Smyrna Beach has a thriving arts scene, with numerous galleries, studios, and theaters. The Atlantic Center for the Arts, a world-renowned artists' residency program, attracts artists from around the globe and hosts a variety of cultural events, workshops, and exhibitions. The city's historic downtown area is home to the New Smyrna Beach Museum of History, which showcases the city's heritage through engaging exhibits and programs.

The city also hosts a variety of festivals and events throughout the year, celebrating everything from seafood and jazz to surfing and art. These events not only provide entertainment for residents and visitors but also foster a strong sense of community and cultural pride.

Michael R. Linton, Author, Real Estate Broker eXp Realty
www.FloridaBeachLife.com

Quality of Life

One of the most appealing aspects of New Smyrna Beach is its quality of life. The city's laid-back atmosphere, friendly community, and abundance of outdoor activities make it an ideal place to live. The cost of living in New Smyrna Beach is relatively affordable compared to other coastal cities in Florida, making it an attractive option for families, retirees, and young professionals.

The city boasts excellent schools, healthcare facilities, and public services. Its proximity to major cities like Orlando and Daytona Beach provides residents with easy access to additional amenities and employment opportunities while allowing them to enjoy the tranquility of coastal living.

FLORIDA BEACH LIFE
New Smyrna Beach Real Estate Guide

Real Estate Overview

The real estate market in New Smyrna Beach is diverse, offering a range of options from charming historic homes and beachfront condos to modern developments and luxury estates. The demand for properties in the area has been steadily increasing, driven by its desirable location, vibrant community, and strong investment potential.

Whether you're looking for a primary residence, a vacation home, or an investment property, New Smyrna Beach offers something for everyone. The following chapters will provide you with detailed insights into the local real estate market, the home buying and selling process, and the investment opportunities available in this beautiful coastal city.

In conclusion, New Smyrna Beach is a unique and vibrant community with a rich history, a thriving arts scene, and a high quality of life. Its stunning natural beauty, diverse recreational opportunities, and strong sense of community make it an ideal place to call home. As you embark on your real estate journey in New Smyrna Beach, this guide will provide you with the knowledge and resources you need to make informed decisions and achieve your real estate goals.

Michael R. Linton, Author, Real Estate Broker eXp Realty
www.FloridaBeachLife.com

Chapter 2: Understanding the Local Real Estate Market

The real estate market in New Smyrna Beach is dynamic and multifaceted, shaped by various factors such as economic trends, demographic shifts, and local developments. Understanding these factors is crucial for making informed decisions whether you are buying, selling, or investing in property. This chapter delves into the key elements that influence the New Smyrna Beach real estate market and provides a comprehensive analysis to help you navigate it effectively.

Market Trends and Statistics

The New Smyrna Beach real estate market has experienced significant growth in recent years, driven by increased demand for coastal properties and a steady influx of new residents. The median home price in New Smyrna Beach has been rising, reflecting the area's desirability and strong investment potential. Understanding these market trends is essential for buyers and sellers to make strategic decisions.

Home Prices and Sales Volume:

- The median home price in New Smyrna Beach has seen consistent growth, with properties appreciating at an average rate of 5-7% annually.
- Sales volume has also increased, with a notable uptick in the number of single-family homes, condos, and townhouses being sold.

FLORIDA BEACH LIFE
New Smyrna Beach Real Estate Guide

- The market has a balanced mix of new constructions and existing homes, catering to various preferences and budgets.

Inventory and Days on Market:

- The inventory of available homes has fluctuated, with periods of high demand leading to lower inventory levels.
- The average days on market for properties in New Smyrna Beach have decreased, indicating a competitive market where homes sell quickly. In some neighborhoods, well-priced homes may receive multiple offers and sell within a few days of listing.

FLORIDA BEACH LIFE
New Smyrna Beach Real Estate Guide

Rental Market:

- The rental market in New Smyrna Beach is robust, driven by demand for both long-term rentals and vacation properties. The area's popularity as a tourist destination ensures a steady stream of short-term rental income for property owners.
- Vacation rentals, particularly those close to the beach, command premium rates, making them an attractive investment option.

Economic and Demographic Factors

Understanding the broader economic and demographic trends impacting New Smyrna Beach is crucial for making informed real estate decisions. These factors influence

FLORIDA BEACH LIFE
New Smyrna Beach Real Estate Guide

housing demand, property values, and investment opportunities.

Population Growth:

- New Smyrna Beach has experienced steady population growth, attracting new residents with its appealing lifestyle and amenities. The city's population is diverse, comprising retirees, families, young professionals, and seasonal residents.
- The influx of new residents has fueled demand for housing, contributing to rising property values.

Economic Development:

FLORIDA BEACH LIFE
New Smyrna Beach Real Estate Guide

- The local economy in New Smyrna Beach is diverse, with significant contributions from tourism, healthcare, education, and retail sectors. The city's thriving tourism industry, bolstered by its beautiful beaches and cultural attractions, plays a pivotal role in driving economic growth.
- Ongoing and planned developments, such as infrastructure improvements, new commercial projects, and community enhancements, further support the local economy and real estate market.

Neighborhood Insights

New Smyrna Beach comprises various neighborhoods, each with its unique character, amenities, and real estate offerings. Understanding the nuances of these neighborhoods is essential for finding the right property that meets your needs and preferences.

Beachside Communities:

- Beachside neighborhoods, such as Flagler Avenue, offer easy access to the beach, vibrant nightlife, and a range of dining and shopping options. These areas are highly sought after by both residents and tourists, making them ideal for investment properties.
- Properties in beachside communities tend to command higher prices due to their prime location and desirable amenities.

Mainland Neighborhoods:

- Mainland neighborhoods, like Venetian Bay and Sugar Mill, offer a mix of single-family homes, townhouses, and condos. These areas are known for their family-friendly environment, excellent schools, and recreational facilities.
- Mainland properties often provide more affordable options compared to beachside communities while still offering convenient access to the city's amenities.

Historic Districts:

- Historic districts, such as the Canal Street Historic District, feature charming older homes with unique architectural styles. These neighborhoods have a strong sense of community and are close to cultural attractions, parks, and the waterfront.

- Investing in historic properties can offer both charm and potential appreciation, particularly if the area undergoes revitalization.

Investment Opportunities

Investing in New Smyrna Beach real estate offers numerous opportunities for generating income and building wealth. Whether you're interested in rental properties, fix-and-flip projects, or long-term investments, understanding the local market dynamics is key to success.

Vacation Rentals:

- Vacation rentals are a popular investment choice in New Smyrna Beach, thanks to the city's steady stream of tourists. Properties close to the beach, with amenities like pools and ocean views, can generate substantial rental income.
- Managing vacation rentals requires a proactive approach, including marketing, maintenance, and guest relations. Many investors choose to work with property management companies to streamline operations.

Long-Term Rentals:

- Long-term rentals provide stable, consistent income and are less management-intensive compared to vacation rentals. New Smyrna Beach's growing population ensures a steady demand for rental properties.

- Key factors to consider when investing in long-term rentals include location, property condition, and tenant screening processes.

Fix-and-Flip:

- The fix-and-flip market in New Smyrna Beach offers opportunities for investors to buy distressed properties, renovate them, and sell for a profit. Success in this market requires a keen eye for potential, strong project management skills, and a network of reliable contractors.

FLORIDA BEACH LIFE
New Smyrna Beach Real Estate Guide

- Understanding the local market trends and buyer preferences is essential to ensure the renovated property appeals to potential buyers.

Commercial Real Estate:

- Commercial real estate in New Smyrna Beach includes retail spaces, office buildings, and mixed-use developments. The city's growing economy and tourist traffic make commercial properties an attractive investment.
- Assessing the location, foot traffic, and potential for growth are crucial when investing in commercial real estate.

Michael R. Linton, Author, Real Estate Broker eXp Realty
www.FloridaBeachLife.com

Future Outlook

The future outlook for New Smyrna Beach's real estate market remains positive, driven by ongoing development, economic growth, and the city's appeal as a desirable place to live and visit.

Development Projects:

- Several development projects are underway in New Smyrna Beach, including infrastructure improvements, new residential communities, and commercial expansions. These projects are expected to enhance the city's amenities and boost property values.

- Keeping an eye on upcoming developments can provide insights into emerging investment opportunities and market trends.

Sustainability and Resilience:

- New Smyrna Beach is committed to sustainability and resilience, with initiatives focused on preserving the natural environment and enhancing the city's infrastructure. These efforts contribute to the long-term attractiveness and stability of the real estate market.
- Investing in properties that align with sustainability goals, such as energy-efficient homes and eco-

friendly developments, can offer additional benefits and appeal to environmentally conscious buyers.

In summary, understanding the local real estate market in New Smyrna Beach involves analyzing market trends, economic factors, neighborhood dynamics, and investment opportunities. By staying informed and leveraging this knowledge, you can make strategic decisions and achieve success in the New Smyrna Beach real estate market.

Chapter 3: Finding Your Perfect Home in New Smyrna Beach

Finding your perfect home in New Smyrna Beach is an exciting journey filled with possibilities. Whether you're looking for a beachfront condo, a historic home, or a modern family residence, this chapter provides a step-by-step guide to help you navigate the home-buying process and make informed decisions.

Identifying Your Needs and Preferences

The first step in finding your perfect home is to identify your needs and preferences. This involves considering various factors such as location, property type, budget, and lifestyle.

Location:

FLORIDA BEACH LIFE
New Smyrna Beach Real Estate Guide

- Decide whether you prefer living on the beachside, mainland, or in a specific neighborhood. Each area offers unique amenities and characteristics.
- Consider proximity to schools, work, recreational facilities, and other important locations.

Property Type:

- Determine the type of property that best suits your needs, such as single-family homes, condos, townhouses, or historic properties.
- Consider the size, layout, and features of the property, including the number of bedrooms and bathrooms, outdoor space, and special amenities.

FLORIDA BEACH LIFE
New Smyrna Beach Real Estate Guide

Budget:

- Establish your budget, taking into account your financial situation, mortgage pre-approval, and additional costs such as property taxes, insurance, and maintenance.
- Understand the price range of properties in your desired location and be prepared to adjust your expectations based on market conditions.

Lifestyle:

- Consider your lifestyle preferences and how they align with different neighborhoods and property types. For example, beachside living may appeal to those who enjoy water sports and a vibrant nightlife, while mainland neighborhoods may be more suitable for families seeking a quiet, suburban environment.

Starting Your Property Search

Once you have a clear understanding of your needs and preferences, you can begin your property search. This involves exploring various resources and leveraging technology to find potential homes.

Online Listings:

- Utilize online real estate platforms to browse property listings, view photos, and compare prices. Websites

FLORIDA BEACH LIFE
New Smyrna Beach Real Estate Guide

like Zillow, Realtor.com, and local real estate agency websites are excellent starting points.

- Set up alerts for new listings that match your criteria to stay informed about available properties.

Real Estate Agents:

- Working with a local real estate agent can significantly enhance your property search. Agents have in-depth knowledge of the market, access to exclusive listings, and can provide valuable insights and guidance.
- Choose an agent with experience in New Smyrna Beach and a strong track record of helping clients find homes.

Michael R. Linton, Author, Real Estate Broker eXp Realty
www.FloridaBeachLife.com

Open Houses and Tours:

- Attend open houses and schedule private tours to view properties in person. This allows you to get a feel for the home, assess its condition, and visualize yourself living there.
- Take notes and photos during tours to help you remember key details and compare properties later.

Evaluating Potential Homes

As you view potential homes, it's essential to evaluate them thoroughly to ensure they meet your needs and expectations. This involves assessing various aspects of the property and considering potential issues.

FLORIDA BEACH LIFE
New Smyrna Beach Real Estate Guide

Property Condition:

- Examine the overall condition of the property, including the exterior, interior, and any structures on the premises. Look for signs of wear and tear, damage, or needed repairs.
- Pay attention to the age and condition of major systems such as the roof, HVAC, plumbing, and electrical systems.

Layout and Features:

- Consider the layout and flow of the home, ensuring it meets your functional needs and preferences.

Evaluate the size and usability of each room and the overall design of the property.

- Take note of any special features or amenities, such as updated kitchens and bathrooms, outdoor living spaces, pools, and waterfront views.

Neighborhood and Surroundings:

- Assess the neighborhood and its surroundings, including the proximity to schools, parks, shopping centers, and public transportation.
- Observe the condition of neighboring properties and the overall ambiance of the community.

Potential Issues:

- Identify any potential issues that may affect your enjoyment or value of the property, such as noise, traffic, flooding, or zoning restrictions.
- Consider the potential for future developments in the area that may impact your property.

Making an Offer

Once you have found a home that meets your criteria, the next step is to make an offer. This involves several key steps and considerations to ensure a successful transaction.

Determining Offer Price:

- Work with your real estate agent to determine a competitive offer price based on the property's market value, recent comparable sales, and your budget.

- Consider the current market conditions, such as whether it's a buyer's or seller's market, and the level of competition for the property.

Drafting the Offer:

- Your real estate agent will help you draft a formal offer letter, which typically includes the offer price, contingencies, earnest money deposit, and proposed closing date.
- Contingencies are conditions that must be met for the sale to proceed, such as securing financing, satisfactory home inspection, and appraisal.

FLORIDA BEACH LIFE
New Smyrna Beach Real Estate Guide

Submitting the Offer:

- Submit the offer to the seller through your real estate agent. The seller can accept, reject, or counter your offer. Be prepared for negotiations and remain flexible.

Negotiations:

- If the seller counters your offer, review the terms carefully and decide whether to accept, reject, or counter again.
- Effective negotiation involves finding a balance between your interests and the seller's needs, aiming for a win-win outcome.

Closing the Deal

Once your offer is accepted, the final steps involve completing the necessary procedures to close the deal. This includes inspections, securing financing, and finalizing the sale.

Home Inspection:

- Schedule a home inspection to identify any issues or needed repairs. The inspection report will provide a detailed assessment of the property's condition.
- Based on the inspection results, you can request repairs, negotiate a price reduction, or, if major issues are found, reconsider your purchase.

FLORIDA BEACH LIFE
New Smyrna Beach Real Estate Guide

Appraisal:

- Your lender will require an appraisal to determine the property's value. The appraisal ensures that the loan amount does not exceed the property's worth.
- If the appraisal comes in lower than the offer price, you may need to renegotiate with the seller or adjust your financing.

Finalizing Financing:

- Complete the mortgage application process, providing all required documentation to your lender. Stay in close communication with your lender to ensure a smooth process.

- Secure homeowner's insurance, which is typically required by lenders before closing.

Closing Process:

- Review the closing disclosure, which outlines the final terms of your loan, including the loan amount, interest rate, monthly payments, and closing costs.
- Conduct a final walk-through of the property to ensure it is in the agreed-upon condition.
- Attend the closing meeting, where you will sign the necessary documents, pay closing costs, and receive the keys to your new home.

Post-Closing:

- After closing, ensure that you change the locks, set up utilities, and notify relevant parties of your new address.
- Familiarize yourself with your new neighborhood and enjoy settling into your new home.

In conclusion, finding your perfect home in New Smyrna Beach involves a thorough understanding of your needs, a strategic property search, careful evaluation of potential homes, effective offer negotiation, and a smooth closing process. By following these steps and leveraging the expertise of your real estate agent, you can navigate the home-buying journey with confidence and achieve your goal of owning a beautiful home in this vibrant coastal community.

Michael R. Linton, Author, Real Estate Broker eXp Realty
www.FloridaBeachLife.com

FLORIDA BEACH LIFE
New Smyrna Beach Real Estate Guide

Chapter 4: Key Neighborhoods and Communities

New Smyrna Beach offers a variety of neighborhoods and communities, each with its unique charm, amenities, and lifestyle. Whether you're looking for a beachfront condo, a historic home, or a family-friendly neighborhood, this chapter explores the key areas of New Smyrna Beach to help you find the perfect place to call home.

Beachside Neighborhoods

Flagler Avenue:

- Flagler Avenue is one of the most popular and vibrant areas in New Smyrna Beach. Known for its lively atmosphere, this neighborhood offers a mix of shops, restaurants, bars, and art galleries.

- The beach is just steps away, making it an ideal location for those who enjoy beach activities and nightlife. Properties here range from charming bungalows to modern condos with ocean views.

North Beach:

- North Beach is a quieter, more residential area compared to Flagler Avenue. It offers a mix of single-family homes, townhouses, and condos.
- The neighborhood is known for its pristine beaches, beautiful parks, and easy access to the Indian River

FLORIDA BEACH LIFE
New Smyrna Beach Real Estate Guide

Lagoon. It's a perfect spot for families and retirees seeking a peaceful coastal lifestyle.

Mainland Neighborhoods

Venetian Bay:

- Venetian Bay is a master-planned community offering a range of amenities, including a golf course, fitness center, swimming pool, and walking trails.
- The neighborhood features a mix of single-family homes, townhouses, and condos. It's an ideal location for families and active adults looking for a community-oriented lifestyle.

Sugar Mill:

Michael R. Linton, Author, Real Estate Broker eXp Realty
www.FloridaBeachLife.com

- Sugar Mill is a well-established neighborhood known for its beautiful homes, lush landscaping, and friendly community.
- The area offers various amenities, including a golf course, tennis courts, and a clubhouse. It's a great place for those who enjoy an active lifestyle and a close-knit community.

Historic Districts

Canal Street Historic District:

- The Canal Street Historic District is known for its charming historic homes, tree-lined streets, and vibrant downtown area.

- The district features a variety of shops, restaurants, and cultural attractions, including the New Smyrna Beach Museum of History. It's an ideal location for those who appreciate history and culture.

Coronado Island:

- Coronado Island offers a mix of historic homes and modern developments, providing a unique blend of old and new.
- The neighborhood is close to the beach, the Indian River Lagoon, and downtown New Smyrna Beach. It's a perfect spot for those seeking a convenient location with a rich history.

FLORIDA BEACH LIFE
New Smyrna Beach Real Estate Guide

Family-Friendly Neighborhoods

Isles of Sugar Mill:

- The Isles of Sugar Mill is a family-friendly neighborhood featuring single-family homes with spacious yards and modern amenities.
- The community offers parks, playgrounds, and excellent schools, making it an ideal place for families with children.

Sabal Lakes:

- Sabal Lakes is a quiet, family-oriented neighborhood with a mix of single-family homes and townhouses.

- The area is known for its friendly community, beautiful parks, and proximity to schools and recreational facilities. It's a great location for families seeking a suburban lifestyle.

Luxury Communities

Inlet Shores:

- Inlet Shores is a prestigious waterfront community offering luxury homes with private docks, stunning views, and direct access to the Intracoastal Waterway.
- The neighborhood is perfect for boating enthusiasts and those seeking a high-end coastal lifestyle.

Bethune Beach:

- Bethune Beach offers luxury beachfront homes with panoramic ocean views and private beach access.
- The community is known for its upscale properties, serene environment, and proximity to the Canaveral National Seashore. It's an ideal location for those seeking exclusivity and natural beauty.

Active Adult Communities

The Preserve at Turnbull Bay:

- The Preserve at Turnbull Bay is an active adult community offering a range of amenities, including a clubhouse, fitness center, and swimming pool.

FLORIDA BEACH LIFE
New Smyrna Beach Real Estate Guide

- The neighborhood features single-family homes and townhouses designed for low-maintenance living. It's a perfect spot for retirees and active adults seeking a vibrant community.

The Palms at Venetian Bay:

- The Palms at Venetian Bay is an active adult community within the larger Venetian Bay development. It offers a variety of amenities, including golf, fitness facilities, and social clubs.
- The neighborhood provides single-family homes and condos with modern features and easy access to community activities. It's an ideal location for those looking to enjoy an active and social lifestyle.

FLORIDA BEACH LIFE
New Smyrna Beach Real Estate Guide

In summary, New Smyrna Beach offers a diverse range of neighborhoods and communities, each with its unique appeal and lifestyle. Whether you're seeking a lively beachside area, a peaceful mainland neighborhood, a historic district, or a luxury community, there's something for everyone in this beautiful coastal city. By exploring these key areas and considering your needs and preferences, you can find the perfect place to call home in New Smyrna Beach.

Chapter 5: Navigating the Home Buying Process

The home buying process in New Smyrna Beach can be an exciting yet complex journey. Understanding each step of the process can help you navigate it smoothly and make informed decisions. This chapter provides a detailed guide to buying a home in New Smyrna Beach, from preparing to buy to closing the deal.

Preparing to Buy

Before you start looking for a home, it's essential to prepare yourself financially and mentally for the home buying process. This involves several key steps:

Assessing Your Financial Situation:

- Review your finances, including your savings, income, and credit score. A strong financial position will help you secure a mortgage and negotiate better terms.
- Determine how much you can afford to spend on a home by considering your budget, down payment, and monthly mortgage payments.

Getting Pre-Approved for a Mortgage:

- Obtain a mortgage pre-approval from a lender, which provides an estimate of how much you can borrow based on your financial situation.
- Pre-approval demonstrates to sellers that you are a serious buyer and can give you an edge in competitive markets.

FLORIDA BEACH LIFE
New Smyrna Beach Real Estate Guide

Saving for a Down Payment:

- Save for a down payment, typically ranging from 3% to 20% of the home's purchase price. A larger down payment can lower your monthly mortgage payments and potentially qualify you for better loan terms.
- Consider additional costs such as closing fees, property taxes, insurance, and moving expenses.

Starting Your Property Search

Once you are financially prepared, you can begin your property search. This involves several key steps:

Defining Your Needs and Preferences:

FLORIDA BEACH LIFE
New Smyrna Beach Real Estate Guide

- Identify your needs and preferences, including location, property type, size, and features.
- Consider factors such as proximity to work, schools, amenities, and lifestyle preferences.

Researching the Market:

- Research the New Smyrna Beach real estate market to understand current trends, property values, and availability.
- Use online real estate platforms to browse listings and set up alerts for new properties that match your criteria.

Working with a Real Estate Agent:

Michael R. Linton, Author, Real Estate Broker eXp Realty
www.FloridaBeachLife.com

- Find a local real estate agent who specializes in the New Smyrna Beach market. An experienced agent can provide valuable insights, access to off-market listings, and expert guidance throughout the buying process.
- Schedule property viewings and attend open houses to get a firsthand look at potential homes.

Making an Offer

When you find a property that meets your criteria, the next step is to make an offer. This involves several key steps:

Determining Offer Price:

- Your real estate agent will help you analyze comparable properties (comps) to determine a fair offer price based on recent sales in the area.
- Consider the property's condition, location, market conditions, and your budget when deciding on an offer price.

Drafting the Offer:

- Your agent will draft a formal offer letter, which includes the offer price, contingencies, earnest money deposit, and proposed closing date.
- Contingencies protect you as a buyer by allowing you to back out of the deal if certain conditions are not

FLORIDA BEACH LIFE
New Smyrna Beach Real Estate Guide

met, such as securing financing, a satisfactory home inspection, or an appraisal.

Submitting the Offer:

- Submit the offer to the seller through your agent. The seller can accept, reject, or counter your offer.
- Be prepared for negotiations and remain flexible to reach a mutually beneficial agreement.

Inspections and Appraisals

Once your offer is accepted, the next steps are inspections and appraisals to ensure the property is in good condition and valued appropriately.

Home Inspection:

- Hire a professional home inspector to assess the property's condition, including the structure, systems, and appliances.
- Review the inspection report and discuss any issues with your agent. You can request repairs, negotiate a price reduction, or withdraw your offer based on the findings.

Appraisal:

- Your lender will require an appraisal to determine the property's market value. The appraisal ensures the loan amount does not exceed the property's worth.

FLORIDA BEACH LIFE
New Smyrna Beach Real Estate Guide

- If the appraisal is lower than the offer price, you may need to renegotiate with the seller or adjust your financing.

Finalizing Financing

Securing financing is a crucial step in the home buying process. This involves several key steps:

Loan Application:

- Complete the mortgage application process, providing all necessary documentation to your lender.
- Stay in close communication with your lender to ensure a smooth process and address any issues promptly.

Michael R. Linton, Author, Real Estate Broker eXp Realty
www.FloridaBeachLife.com

Homeowner's Insurance:

- Obtain homeowner's insurance, which is typically required by lenders before closing. Insurance protects your investment and covers potential damages or losses.

Reviewing Closing Disclosure:

- Review the closing disclosure, which outlines the final terms of your loan, including the loan amount, interest rate, monthly payments, and closing costs.
- Ensure all information is accurate and matches your expectations.

FLORIDA BEACH LIFE
New Smyrna Beach Real Estate Guide

Closing the Deal

The final step in the home buying process is closing the deal. This involves several key steps:

Final Walk-Through:

- Conduct a final walk-through of the property to ensure it is in the agreed-upon condition and any requested repairs have been completed.
- Verify that all included appliances and fixtures are present and functioning.

Closing Meeting:

FLORIDA BEACH LIFE
New Smyrna Beach Real Estate Guide

- Attend the closing meeting, where you will sign the necessary documents, pay closing costs, and receive the keys to your new home.
- Closing costs typically include fees for the loan, title insurance, property taxes, and recording the deed.

Post-Closing:

- After closing, change the locks, set up utilities, and notify relevant parties of your new address.
- Familiarize yourself with your new neighborhood and enjoy settling into your new home.

In conclusion, navigating the home buying process in New Smyrna Beach requires careful planning, financial preparation, and expert guidance. By following these steps and leveraging the expertise of your real estate agent, you can successfully find and purchase your dream home in this beautiful coastal community.

Michael R. Linton, Author, Real Estate Broker eXp Realty
www.FloridaBeachLife.com

Chapter 6: Financing Your New Home

Securing financing is a critical step in the home buying process. This chapter provides a comprehensive guide to understanding your financing options, preparing for the mortgage application process, and managing your finances effectively.

Understanding Mortgage Options

There are various mortgage options available to homebuyers. Understanding the different types of mortgages can help you choose the best option for your financial situation.

Conventional Loans:

- Conventional loans are not insured or guaranteed by the federal government. They typically require a higher credit score and a larger down payment but offer competitive interest rates.
- Conventional loans can be fixed-rate or adjustable-rate, depending on your preference and financial goals.

FHA Loans:

- FHA loans are insured by the Federal Housing Administration and are designed for first-time homebuyers or those with lower credit scores.

- They require a smaller down payment (as low as 3.5%) and have more lenient credit requirements, making them accessible to a broader range of buyers.

VA Loans:

- VA loans are available to eligible veterans, active-duty service members, and their families. These loans are guaranteed by the Department of Veterans Affairs and typically require no down payment.
- VA loans offer competitive interest rates and do not require private mortgage insurance (PMI).

USDA Loans:

- USDA loans are designed for buyers in rural and suburban areas. These loans are guaranteed by the U.S. Department of Agriculture and typically require no down payment.
- They are intended for low-to-moderate-income buyers and offer competitive interest rates.

Preparing for the Mortgage Application

Before applying for a mortgage, it's essential to prepare yourself financially and gather the necessary documentation. This involves several key steps:

Reviewing Your Credit Report:

FLORIDA BEACH LIFE
New Smyrna Beach Real Estate Guide

- Obtain a copy of your credit report from the major credit bureaus (Equifax, Experian, and TransUnion) and review it for accuracy.
- Address any errors or discrepancies, and take steps to improve your credit score, such as paying down debt and making timely payments.

Gathering Documentation:

- Lenders will require various documents to verify your financial situation, including proof of income (pay stubs, tax returns), assets (bank statements, investment accounts), and debts (loan statements, credit card balances).

- Having these documents ready can expedite the mortgage application process and demonstrate your financial stability.

Determining Your Budget:

- Calculate how much you can afford to spend on a home by considering your income, expenses, and financial goals.
- Use online mortgage calculators to estimate your monthly mortgage payments based on different loan amounts, interest rates, and down payment scenarios.

Choosing a Lender

Choosing the right lender is crucial to securing favorable loan terms and a smooth financing process. This involves several key steps:

Researching Lenders:

- Research different lenders, including banks, credit unions, mortgage brokers, and online lenders. Compare their loan products, interest rates, fees, and customer reviews.
- Consider getting pre-approved by multiple lenders to compare offers and negotiate better terms.

Asking Questions:

FLORIDA BEACH LIFE
New Smyrna Beach Real Estate Guide

- Ask potential lenders about their loan products, application process, closing timeline, and any fees or costs associated with the loan.
- Ensure you understand the terms and conditions of the loan, including the interest rate, loan term, and any prepayment penalties.

Evaluating Loan Estimates:

- Review the loan estimates provided by lenders, which outline the estimated costs, interest rates, and monthly payments for the loan.
- Compare the loan estimates to determine which lender offers the best terms for your financial situation.

Managing Your Finances During the Home Buying Process

Managing your finances effectively during the home buying process is crucial to ensuring a smooth transaction and securing favorable loan terms. This involves several key steps:

Maintaining Financial Stability:

- Avoid making significant financial changes, such as changing jobs, making large purchases, or taking on new debt, during the mortgage application process.
- Maintain a stable income and manage your expenses to demonstrate financial responsibility to lenders.

Saving for Closing Costs:

- In addition to the down payment, you will need to save for closing costs, which typically range from 2% to 5% of the home's purchase price.
- Closing costs include fees for the loan, appraisal, title insurance, property taxes, and recording the deed.

Building an Emergency Fund:

- Establish an emergency fund to cover unexpected expenses, such as home repairs, medical bills, or job loss.
- Aim to save at least three to six months' worth of living expenses in a separate savings account.

In summary, securing financing for your new home in New Smyrna Beach involves understanding your mortgage options, preparing for the application process, choosing the right lender, and managing your finances effectively. By following these steps and working with a knowledgeable real estate agent and lender, you can navigate the financing process with confidence and achieve your goal of homeownership in this beautiful coastal community.

Chapter 7: Selling Your Property

Selling a property in New Smyrna Beach requires careful planning, strategic marketing, and effective negotiation. This chapter provides a comprehensive guide to selling your home, from preparing your property for sale to closing the deal.

Preparing Your Property for Sale

Before listing your property, it's essential to prepare it for sale to attract potential buyers and maximize its market value. This involves several key steps:

Assessing Your Property:

- Conduct a thorough assessment of your property to identify any necessary repairs or improvements.
- Consider getting a pre-listing home inspection to uncover any issues that may need to be addressed before listing.

Making Repairs and Improvements:

- Complete any necessary repairs, such as fixing leaky faucets, repairing damaged walls, and addressing electrical or plumbing issues.
- Consider making cosmetic improvements, such as painting, updating fixtures, and enhancing curb appeal, to make your property more attractive to buyers.

FLORIDA BEACH LIFE
New Smyrna Beach Real Estate Guide

Staging Your Home:

- Stage your home to showcase its best features and create a welcoming atmosphere for potential buyers.
- Declutter and depersonalize your space, arrange furniture to highlight the layout, and add tasteful decor to enhance the overall appeal.

Setting the Right Price

Pricing your property correctly is crucial to attracting buyers and achieving a successful sale. This involves several key steps:

Analyzing the Market:

FLORIDA BEACH LIFE
New Smyrna Beach Real Estate Guide

- Research the local real estate market to understand current trends, including recent sales of comparable properties (comps), average days on market, and the supply-demand balance.

- Use this data to determine a competitive listing price that reflects your property's value and attracts potential buyers.

Working with Your Real Estate Agent:

- Collaborate with your real estate agent to set the right price. An experienced agent will provide a comparative market analysis (CMA) and expert advice on pricing strategies.

- Be open to adjusting your price based on market feedback and the initial response from buyers.

Marketing Your Property

Effective marketing is essential to reach potential buyers and generate interest in your property. This involves several key steps:

Professional Photography:

- Invest in professional photography to capture high-quality images of your property. Attractive photos can significantly enhance your listing and draw more attention online.

- Consider virtual tours or video walkthroughs to provide a comprehensive view of your property for remote buyers.

Online Listings:

- List your property on popular real estate platforms such as Zillow, Realtor.com, and the Multiple Listing Service (MLS). Ensure your listing includes detailed descriptions, high-quality photos, and key features.
- Utilize social media to promote your listing and reach a broader audience.

Open Houses and Showings:

FLORIDA BEACH LIFE
New Smyrna Beach Real Estate Guide

- Host open houses to allow potential buyers to tour your property in person. Promote open houses through online listings, social media, and local advertising.
- Schedule private showings for interested buyers and ensure your home is clean, well-staged, and welcoming.

Print Advertising:

- Consider print advertising in local newspapers, real estate magazines, and community newsletters to reach potential buyers who prefer traditional media.
- Use eye-catching flyers and brochures to provide detailed information about your property.

Negotiating Offers

Once you receive offers, the negotiation process begins.

This involves several key steps:

Reviewing Offers:

- Review each offer carefully with your real estate agent, considering factors such as offer price, contingencies, financing, and proposed closing date.
- Evaluate the buyer's qualifications, including their pre-approval status and financial stability.

Counteroffers:

- If an offer is not acceptable, you can respond with a counteroffer, adjusting terms such as price, contingencies, or closing date.
- Be prepared for back-and-forth negotiations to reach an agreement that satisfies both parties.

Accepting an Offer:

- Once you accept an offer, sign the purchase agreement, and notify all parties involved. The buyer will typically provide an earnest money deposit to demonstrate their commitment.
- Work with your agent to ensure all contingencies are met and the transaction progresses smoothly.

FLORIDA BEACH LIFE
New Smyrna Beach Real Estate Guide

Closing the Sale

The final step in selling your property is closing the sale. This involves several key steps:

Home Inspection and Appraisal:

- The buyer will schedule a home inspection and appraisal as part of the contingency process. Address any issues identified in the inspection report and negotiate repairs if necessary.
- Ensure the property appraises at or above the agreed-upon sale price to avoid financing complications.

Preparing for Closing:

FLORIDA BEACH LIFE
New Smyrna Beach Real Estate Guide

- Gather all necessary documents for closing, including the property deed, title report, and any repair receipts.
- Review the closing disclosure, which outlines the final terms of the sale, including the purchase price, closing costs, and any credits or adjustments.

Closing Meeting:

- Attend the closing meeting, where you will sign the necessary documents to transfer ownership to the buyer. The buyer will provide the remaining funds, and you will receive the proceeds from the sale.
- Hand over the keys and any relevant information about the property to the new owner.

Michael R. Linton, Author, Real Estate Broker eXp Realty
www.FloridaBeachLife.com

Post-Closing:

- Cancel any utilities, insurance, and other services in your name effective from the closing date.
- Notify relevant parties, such as your lender, insurance company, and the local tax assessor, of the sale.

In conclusion, selling your property in New Smyrna Beach involves careful preparation, effective marketing, strategic pricing, and successful negotiation. By following these steps and working with a knowledgeable real estate agent, you can navigate the selling process smoothly and achieve a successful sale.

Chapter 8: Marketing Strategies for Sellers

Effective marketing is crucial for selling your property quickly and at the best possible price. This chapter provides a comprehensive guide to marketing your home in New Smyrna Beach, covering traditional and digital strategies, staging tips, and how to leverage your real estate agent's expertise.

Creating a Marketing Plan

A well-thought-out marketing plan is essential for reaching potential buyers and showcasing your property's unique features. This involves several key steps:

Identifying Your Target Audience:

- Determine the type of buyer who would be interested in your property, such as first-time homebuyers, families, retirees, or investors.
- Tailor your marketing efforts to appeal to your target audience, highlighting features and amenities that would attract them.

Setting a Marketing Budget:

- Allocate a budget for marketing activities, including professional photography, online listings, print advertising, and staging.
- Discuss your budget with your real estate agent to ensure it aligns with your marketing goals.

FLORIDA BEACH LIFE
New Smyrna Beach Real Estate Guide

Professional Photography and Staging

High-quality visuals and a well-staged home can significantly impact potential buyers' first impressions. This involves several key steps:

Professional Photography:

- Hire a professional photographer to take high-quality photos of your property. Ensure the photos showcase your home's best features and highlight key areas such as the kitchen, living room, and outdoor spaces.
- Consider virtual tours or video walkthroughs to provide a comprehensive view of your property for remote buyers.

Michael R. Linton, Author, Real Estate Broker eXp Realty
www.FloridaBeachLife.com

Home Staging:

- Stage your home to create a welcoming and appealing environment for potential buyers. Focus on decluttering, depersonalizing, and arranging furniture to highlight the home's layout and features.
- Use neutral colors and tasteful decor to appeal to a broad range of buyers. Consider hiring a professional stager for expert advice and execution.

Digital Marketing Strategies

Digital marketing is essential for reaching a wide audience and generating interest in your property. This involves several key steps:

FLORIDA BEACH LIFE
New Smyrna Beach Real Estate Guide

Online Listings:

- List your property on popular real estate platforms such as Zillow, Realtor.com, and the Multiple Listing Service (MLS). Ensure your listing includes detailed descriptions, high-quality photos, and key features.
- Set up alerts for new listings that match your criteria to stay informed about available properties.

Social Media Marketing:

- Utilize social media platforms such as Facebook, Instagram, and Twitter to promote your property. Share high-quality photos, virtual tours, and updates about open houses.

Michael R. Linton, Author, Real Estate Broker eXp Realty
www.FloridaBeachLife.com

- Engage with potential buyers and respond to inquiries promptly to build interest and trust.

Email Marketing:

- Create an email marketing campaign to reach potential buyers and keep them informed about your property. Include high-quality photos, property details, and information about open houses.
- Use targeted email lists to reach specific buyer segments, such as first-time homebuyers, investors, or retirees.

Traditional Marketing Strategies

FLORIDA BEACH LIFE
New Smyrna Beach Real Estate Guide

While digital marketing is crucial, traditional marketing methods can also be effective in reaching potential buyers. This involves several key steps:

Print Advertising:

- Advertise your property in local newspapers, real estate magazines, and community newsletters. Use eye-catching flyers and brochures to provide detailed information about your property.
- Distribute flyers and brochures in high-traffic areas, such as grocery stores, community centers, and local businesses.

Open Houses and Showings:

- Host open houses to allow potential buyers to tour your property in person. Promote open houses through online listings, social media, and local advertising.
- Schedule private showings for interested buyers and ensure your home is clean, well-staged, and welcoming.

Leveraging Your Real Estate Agent's Expertise

Your real estate agent can provide valuable expertise and resources to enhance your marketing efforts. This involves several key steps:

Collaborating on Marketing Strategies:

- Work closely with your agent to develop and execute a comprehensive marketing plan. Leverage their knowledge of the local market and buyer preferences to tailor your marketing efforts.
- Take advantage of your agent's network of contacts, including other agents, potential buyers, and marketing professionals.

Utilizing Professional Resources:

- Your agent can provide access to professional resources, such as photographers, stagers, and marketing specialists, to enhance your property's appeal.

- Use your agent's expertise to navigate the complexities of the selling process, including pricing, negotiations, and closing.

In conclusion, effective marketing is crucial for selling your property in New Smyrna Beach. By creating a comprehensive marketing plan, utilizing professional photography and staging, leveraging digital and traditional marketing strategies, and collaborating with your real estate agent, you can reach a wide audience and achieve a successful sale.

Chapter 9: Investing in New Smyrna Beach Real Estate

Investing in New Smyrna Beach real estate offers numerous opportunities for generating income and building wealth. This chapter provides a comprehensive guide to understanding the local rental market, evaluating investment properties, and managing your real estate investments effectively.

Understanding the Rental Market

The rental market in New Smyrna Beach is diverse, with demand for both long-term rentals and vacation properties. Understanding the local rental market is crucial for making informed investment decisions.

FLORIDA BEACH LIFE
New Smyrna Beach Real Estate Guide

Long-Term Rentals:

- Long-term rentals provide stable, consistent income and are less management-intensive compared to vacation rentals. The growing population in New Smyrna Beach ensures a steady demand for rental properties.
- Key factors to consider when investing in long-term rentals include location, property condition, and tenant screening processes.

Vacation Rentals:

- Vacation rentals are a popular investment choice in New Smyrna Beach, thanks to the city's steady stream of tourists. Properties close to the beach, with amenities like pools and ocean views, can generate substantial rental income.

- Managing vacation rentals requires a proactive approach, including marketing, maintenance, and guest relations. Many investors choose to work with property management companies to streamline operations.

Evaluating Investment Properties

Evaluating potential investment properties involves analyzing various factors to ensure they meet your financial goals and offer strong returns.

Location:

- he location of the property is a critical factor in its potential for rental income and long-term appreciation. Properties near the beach, downtown areas, or popular attractions tend to have higher demand and rental rates.
- Consider the neighborhood's safety, amenities, and accessibility to essential services such as schools, shopping centers, and public transportation.

Property Condition:

- Assess the property's current condition and any potential renovation or maintenance needs. A well-maintained property attracts quality tenants and reduces ongoing maintenance costs.

- Factor in the cost of any necessary repairs or upgrades when evaluating the overall investment potential.

Rental Income Potential:

- Research the local rental rates for similar properties in the area to estimate the potential rental income. Consider both peak and off-season rates for vacation rentals.
- Calculate the expected cash flow by subtracting operating expenses, such as property management fees, maintenance, insurance, and property taxes, from the rental income.

Return on Investment (ROI):

- Determine the property's ROI by calculating the net annual income (rental income minus expenses) and dividing it by the total investment cost (purchase price plus any renovation costs).
- Aim for properties with a high ROI to ensure a profitable investment.

Financing Investment Properties

Securing financing for investment properties requires careful planning and understanding of the available options. This involves several key steps:

Mortgage Options:

- Explore different mortgage options for investment properties, including conventional loans, portfolio loans, and commercial real estate loans.
- Investment property loans typically require a larger down payment (20-25%) and have higher interest rates compared to primary residence loans.

Pre-Approval Process:

- Obtain a mortgage pre-approval to determine how much you can borrow and to demonstrate to sellers that you are a serious buyer.
- Gather necessary documentation, such as proof of income, assets, and credit history, to expedite the pre-approval process.

Alternative Financing:

- Consider alternative financing options such as hard money loans, private lenders, or real estate investment partnerships if traditional financing is not available or suitable for your investment strategy.
- Evaluate the terms and conditions of alternative financing to ensure they align with your investment goals.

Managing Your Investment Properties

Effective property management is essential for maximizing rental income and maintaining the value of your investment. This involves several key steps:

Property Management:

- Decide whether to manage the property yourself or hire a professional property management company. Property management companies can handle tenant screening, rent collection, maintenance, and marketing.
- Weigh the cost of property management services against the potential benefits, such as reduced stress and professional expertise.

Tenant Screening:

FLORIDA BEACH LIFE
New Smyrna Beach Real Estate Guide

- Implement a thorough tenant screening process to select reliable tenants who will pay rent on time and take care of the property.
- Conduct background checks, credit checks, and reference checks to evaluate potential tenants' financial stability and rental history.

Maintenance and Repairs:

- Regular maintenance and timely repairs are crucial for keeping your property in good condition and ensuring tenant satisfaction.
- Create a maintenance schedule and budget for routine tasks such as landscaping, HVAC servicing, and plumbing inspections.

Marketing and Leasing:

- Develop effective marketing strategies to attract potential tenants, including online listings, social media, and local advertising.
- Clearly outline lease terms, including rent amount, security deposit, lease duration, and property rules, to avoid misunderstandings and disputes.

Legal and Tax Considerations

Understanding the legal and tax implications of real estate investing is crucial for compliance and optimizing your investment returns.

Legal Compliance:

- Familiarize yourself with local, state, and federal regulations regarding rental properties, including tenant rights, lease agreements, and property maintenance standards.
- Consult with a real estate attorney to ensure your lease agreements and property management practices comply with applicable laws.

Tax Benefits and Obligations:

- Real estate investments offer various tax benefits, including deductions for mortgage interest, property taxes, operating expenses, depreciation, and repairs.

- Work with a tax professional to maximize your tax benefits and ensure you meet all tax obligations, including reporting rental income and capital gains.

Exit Strategies

Having a clear exit strategy is essential for maximizing your investment returns and achieving your long-term financial goals.

Selling the Property:

- Monitor the real estate market to identify favorable conditions for selling your investment property. Consider factors such as market trends, property appreciation, and demand.

- Work with a real estate agent to market your property effectively and negotiate the best possible sale price.

1031 Exchange:

- Consider using a 1031 exchange to defer capital gains taxes when selling an investment property and reinvesting the proceeds into a new property.
- Consult with a tax professional to ensure you meet the requirements and deadlines for a 1031 exchange.

Refinancing:

- Refinancing your investment property can provide access to equity for further investments or reduce your monthly mortgage payments.

- Evaluate the costs and benefits of refinancing to determine if it aligns with your investment strategy.

In conclusion, investing in New Smyrna Beach real estate offers numerous opportunities for generating income and building wealth. By understanding the local rental market, evaluating investment properties, securing financing, and effectively managing your investments, you can achieve success in this dynamic and rewarding market. Working with experienced professionals and staying informed about market trends and legal considerations will further enhance your investment outcomes.

Chapter 10: Vacation Rentals and Short-Term Leasing

Vacation rentals and short-term leasing can be lucrative investment opportunities in New Smyrna Beach, given its popularity as a tourist destination. This chapter provides a comprehensive guide to understanding the vacation rental market, managing short-term rentals, and maximizing your rental income.

Understanding the Vacation Rental Market

The vacation rental market in New Smyrna Beach is thriving, driven by the city's beautiful beaches, cultural attractions, and year-round events. Understanding this market is crucial for making informed investment decisions.

FLORIDA BEACH LIFE
New Smyrna Beach Real Estate Guide

Market Demand:

- New Smyrna Beach attracts a diverse range of visitors, including families, couples, and groups of friends, creating strong demand for vacation rentals.
- Peak rental seasons typically include spring break, summer months, and holidays, while the off-season may see reduced demand.

Property Types:

- Vacation rental properties in New Smyrna Beach range from beachfront condos and cottages to larger single-family homes and luxury estates.

FLORIDA BEACH LIFE
New Smyrna Beach Real Estate Guide

- Consider the preferences of your target audience when selecting a property, such as proximity to the beach, amenities, and size.

Setting Up Your Vacation Rental

Setting up your vacation rental property involves several key steps to ensure it appeals to guests and provides a comfortable, enjoyable stay.

Furnishing and Decorating:

- Furnish your property with comfortable, durable furniture and provide essential amenities such as a fully equipped kitchen, high-quality linens, and modern electronics.

- Decorate the property with a cohesive, inviting style that reflects the coastal ambiance of New Smyrna Beach.

Stocking Essentials:

- Provide guests with essential items, including toiletries, kitchen supplies, cleaning products, and basic pantry staples.
- Consider adding extra touches such as beach towels, chairs, and umbrellas to enhance the guest experience.

Safety and Security:

- Ensure the property meets safety standards, including functioning smoke detectors, fire extinguishers, and secure locks.
- Provide clear instructions for emergency procedures and local contact information for guests.

Marketing Your Vacation Rental

Effective marketing is essential for attracting guests and maximizing your rental income. This involves several key steps:

Creating an Attractive Listing:

- Create a compelling listing with high-quality photos, detailed descriptions, and a list of amenities and nearby attractions.
- Highlight unique features such as ocean views, private pools, or proximity to popular destinations.

Utilizing Online Platforms:

- List your property on popular vacation rental platforms such as Airbnb, VRBO, and Booking.com to reach a wide audience.
- Use the platform's tools to manage bookings, communicate with guests, and collect payments.

Leveraging Social Media:

- Promote your vacation rental on social media platforms such as Facebook, Instagram, and Twitter. Share photos, guest reviews, and special promotions to engage potential guests.
- Create a dedicated social media page for your rental property to build a following and increase visibility.

Managing Bookings and Guest Relations

Effective management of bookings and guest relations is crucial for ensuring a positive guest experience and generating repeat business.

Booking Management:

- Use vacation rental management software to streamline bookings, track availability, and automate guest communications.
- Set competitive pricing based on seasonal demand, local events, and market trends. Consider offering discounts for longer stays or off-season bookings.

Guest Communication:

- Communicate promptly and professionally with guests before, during, and after their stay. Provide clear check-in and check-out instructions, house rules, and local recommendations.
- Address any issues or concerns promptly to ensure a positive guest experience.

Cleaning and Maintenance:

- Ensure the property is thoroughly cleaned and well-maintained between guest stays. Hire professional cleaning services if needed.
- Regularly inspect the property for any maintenance issues and address them promptly to avoid guest complaints.

Legal and Regulatory Considerations

Understanding the legal and regulatory requirements for vacation rentals is essential for compliance and avoiding potential issues.

Local Regulations:

- Familiarize yourself with local regulations regarding short-term rentals, including zoning laws, licensing requirements, and occupancy limits.
- Ensure your property complies with all local ordinances and obtain any necessary permits or licenses.

Tax Obligations:

- Understand your tax obligations for vacation rental income, including state and local taxes, transient occupancy taxes, and federal income taxes.
- Work with a tax professional to ensure you meet all tax requirements and take advantage of any available deductions.

FLORIDA BEACH LIFE
New Smyrna Beach Real Estate Guide

Maximizing Rental Income

Maximizing your rental income involves strategic pricing, exceptional guest experiences, and continuous improvement of your property.

Dynamic Pricing:

- Implement dynamic pricing strategies to adjust rental rates based on demand, seasonality, and local events. Use pricing tools and market data to set competitive rates.
- Consider offering special promotions, last-minute deals, and discounts for extended stays to attract more bookings.

Enhancing Guest Experience:

- Provide exceptional guest experiences to encourage positive reviews and repeat bookings. Offer personalized touches such as welcome baskets, local guides, and recommendations for activities and dining.
- Respond promptly to guest inquiries and feedback, showing that you value their stay and are committed to their satisfaction.

Continuous Improvement:

- Regularly update and maintain your property to keep it in top condition. Invest in upgrades that enhance guest comfort and appeal, such as modern appliances, smart home technology, and attractive landscaping.

- Solicit feedback from guests to identify areas for improvement and address any recurring issues.

Working with Property Management Companies

Managing a vacation rental can be time-consuming and complex. Working with a property management company can help streamline operations and maximize your investment.

Benefits of Property Management:

- Property management companies handle various aspects of vacation rental management, including marketing, booking, guest communication, cleaning, and maintenance.
- They provide professional expertise and resources to enhance the guest experience and optimize rental income.

Choosing a Property Management Company:

- Research and interview several property management companies to find one that aligns with your goals and offers the services you need.

- Consider their experience, reputation, fees, and the range of services they provide. Ask for references and read reviews from other property owners.

Contract and Fees:

- Review the management contract carefully to understand the terms, fees, and responsibilities. Management fees typically range from 20% to 30% of the rental income.
- Ensure the contract includes provisions for regular reporting, communication, and accountability.

In conclusion, vacation rentals and short-term leasing in New Smyrna Beach offer lucrative investment opportunities. By understanding the local rental market, setting up and marketing your property effectively, managing bookings and guest relations, complying with legal requirements, and considering property management services, you can maximize your rental income and achieve success in this dynamic market.

Chapter 11: Legal Considerations in New Smyrna Beach Real Estate

Navigating the legal aspects of real estate transactions is crucial for protecting your interests and ensuring a smooth process. This chapter provides a comprehensive guide to understanding the legal considerations involved in buying, selling, and investing in New Smyrna Beach real estate.

Understanding Real Estate Contracts

Real estate contracts are legally binding agreements that outline the terms and conditions of a property transaction. Understanding these contracts is essential for a successful transaction.

Purchase Agreement:

FLORIDA BEACH LIFE
New Smyrna Beach Real Estate Guide

- The purchase agreement is the primary contract between the buyer and seller, detailing the terms of the sale, including the purchase price, contingencies, and closing date.
- Ensure the agreement is thorough and includes all necessary provisions to protect your interests. Consult with a real estate attorney to review and negotiate the contract.

Contingencies:

- Contingencies are conditions that must be met for the sale to proceed. Common contingencies include financing, home inspection, appraisal, and the sale of the buyer's current home.

- Clearly outline all contingencies in the purchase agreement and understand the implications if they are not met.

Disclosures:

- Sellers are required to disclose known defects and issues with the property. Common disclosures include lead-based paint, water damage, mold, and structural problems.
- Ensure you understand the disclosure requirements and provide all necessary information to avoid legal issues.

Title and Escrow

Title and escrow services are essential components of real estate transactions, ensuring that the transfer of ownership is legal and secure.

Title Search:

- A title search is conducted to verify the property's ownership history and ensure there are no liens, encumbrances, or other issues that could affect the transfer of ownership.
- Work with a reputable title company to conduct a thorough title search and obtain title insurance to protect against potential claims.

Escrow Services:

- Escrow is a neutral third-party service that holds funds and documents during the transaction until all conditions are met. This ensures a secure and orderly transfer of ownership.
- Choose a reliable escrow company to manage the process and safeguard your interests.

Closing Process

The closing process finalizes the real estate transaction, transferring ownership from the seller to the buyer. Understanding the steps involved is crucial for a smooth closing.

Reviewing Closing Documents:

FLORIDA BEACH LIFE
New Smyrna Beach Real Estate Guide

- Carefully review all closing documents, including the closing disclosure, deed, and settlement statement. Ensure all information is accurate and matches the terms agreed upon in the purchase agreement.
- Consult with a real estate attorney or your agent to clarify any questions or concerns.

Closing Costs:

- Closing costs typically include fees for the loan, appraisal, title insurance, escrow services, property taxes, and recording the deed. These costs are usually shared between the buyer and seller.
- Understand the breakdown of closing costs and be prepared to pay your share at closing.

Michael R. Linton, Author, Real Estate Broker eXp Realty
www.FloridaBeachLife.com

Signing and Finalizing:

- Attend the closing meeting to sign all necessary documents and complete the transaction. Both the buyer and seller (or their representatives) must be present.
- Once all documents are signed and funds are transferred, the title and keys are handed over to the buyer, finalizing the sale.

Land Use and Zoning Regulations

Land use and zoning regulations govern how properties can be used and developed. Understanding these regulations is crucial for ensuring compliance and maximizing your property's potential.

FLORIDA BEACH LIFE
New Smyrna Beach Real Estate Guide

Zoning Laws:

- Zoning laws classify properties into categories such as residential, commercial, industrial, and mixed-use. Each category has specific regulations regarding property use, building size, and setbacks.
- Check the zoning classification of your property and any planned developments to ensure compliance with local regulations.

Permits and Approvals:

- Construction, renovations, and certain property uses may require permits and approvals from local authorities. This includes building permits, occupancy permits, and special use permits.

- Obtain all necessary permits and approvals before starting any work to avoid fines and legal issues.

Landlord-Tenant Laws

If you plan to rent out your property, understanding landlord-tenant laws is essential for managing your rental property legally and effectively.

Lease Agreements:

- A lease agreement is a contract between the landlord and tenant, outlining the terms and conditions of the rental. This includes rent amount, lease duration, security deposit, and property rules.

- Ensure your lease agreement is comprehensive and complies with local and state laws. Consider having it reviewed by a real estate attorney.

Tenant Rights and Responsibilities:

- Tenants have rights regarding habitability, privacy, and non-discrimination. They are also responsible for paying rent on time, maintaining the property, and adhering to lease terms.
- Familiarize yourself with tenant rights and ensure you provide a safe and habitable living environment.

Eviction Procedures:

- Eviction is a legal process to remove a tenant from your property for violating lease terms, such as non-payment of rent or property damage. The process must be carried out in accordance with local laws.
- Follow the proper legal procedures for eviction to avoid potential legal issues and ensure a fair process.

Working with a Real Estate Attorney

A real estate attorney can provide valuable legal guidance and representation throughout the buying, selling, and investing process.

Legal Advice and Representation:

- A real estate attorney can help review and negotiate contracts, resolve disputes, and ensure compliance with local laws and regulations.
- Choose an attorney with experience in New Smyrna Beach real estate to provide expert advice tailored to your needs.

Drafting and Reviewing Documents:

- Attorneys can draft and review legal documents, including purchase agreements, lease agreements, and closing documents, to protect your interests and ensure accuracy.
- Having an attorney review documents can prevent potential legal issues and provide peace of mind.

FLORIDA BEACH LIFE
New Smyrna Beach Real Estate Guide

In conclusion, navigating the legal considerations of New Smyrna Beach real estate requires a thorough understanding of contracts, title and escrow services, the closing process, land use regulations, landlord-tenant laws, and the benefits of working with a real estate attorney. By staying informed and seeking professional legal guidance, you can protect your interests and ensure a successful real estate transaction.

Chapter 12: Working with Real Estate Agents

A knowledgeable and experienced real estate agent can be a valuable asset in buying, selling, and investing in New Smyrna Beach real estate. This chapter provides a comprehensive guide to choosing and working with real estate agents to achieve your real estate goals.

Choosing the Right Real Estate Agent

Selecting the right real estate agent is crucial for a successful transaction. Consider the following factors when choosing an agent:

Experience and Expertise:

- Look for an agent with extensive experience in the New Smyrna Beach market. An experienced agent will have a deep understanding of local market trends, property values, and neighborhood dynamics.
- Consider agents who specialize in your specific needs, such as first-time homebuyers, luxury properties, or investment properties.

Reputation and References:

- Research the agent's reputation by reading online reviews, checking their website, and asking for references from past clients.

FLORIDA BEACH LIFE
New Smyrna Beach Real Estate Guide

- Speak with references to get a sense of the agent's communication style, professionalism, and success rate.

Professional Credentials:

- Verify the agent's professional credentials, including their real estate license and any additional certifications or designations (e.g., Certified Residential Specialist, Accredited Buyer's Representative).
- Membership in professional organizations, such as the National Association of Realtors (NAR), indicates a commitment to ethical standards and ongoing education.

FLORIDA BEACH LIFE
New Smyrna Beach Real Estate Guide

Communicating Effectively with Your Agent

Effective communication with your real estate agent is essential for a smooth and successful transaction. Consider the following tips:

Setting Expectations:

- Clearly communicate your goals, preferences, and budget to your agent. Provide specific details about what you're looking for in a property or what you expect from the sale.
- Discuss your preferred communication methods and frequency of updates to ensure you stay informed throughout the process.

Michael R. Linton, Author, Real Estate Broker eXp Realty
www.FloridaBeachLife.com

FLORIDA BEACH LIFE
New Smyrna Beach Real Estate Guide

Providing Feedback:

- Provide timely and constructive feedback to your agent during property showings, negotiations, and the closing process. This helps your agent tailor their approach to better meet your needs.
- Be open and honest about any concerns or issues that arise, allowing your agent to address them promptly.

Listening to Advice:

- Trust your agent's expertise and listen to their advice on market conditions, pricing strategies, and

negotiation tactics. They have the experience and knowledge to guide you through the process.
- Be open to their suggestions, even if they differ from your initial expectations. An experienced agent can provide valuable insights that can lead to a more successful transaction.

Leveraging Your Agent's Resources

Real estate agents have access to a wide range of resources and tools that can enhance your buying or selling experience. Utilize these resources to your advantage:

Market Analysis:

- Your agent can provide a comprehensive market analysis, including recent sales data, market trends, and property values in your desired area. This information is crucial for making informed decisions.
- Use the market analysis to set realistic expectations for pricing, whether you're buying or selling a property.

Property Listings:

- Agents have access to the Multiple Listing Service (MLS), which includes detailed information on available properties. This gives you access to a broader range of listings than public websites.

- Your agent can set up alerts for new listings that match your criteria, ensuring you stay informed about potential opportunities.

Networking and Contacts:

- Real estate agents have extensive networks of industry professionals, including mortgage brokers, home inspectors, contractors, and attorneys. These contacts can be invaluable throughout the transaction process.
- Leverage your agent's network to find reliable professionals who can assist with various aspects of buying, selling, or investing in real estate.

FLORIDA BEACH LIFE
New Smyrna Beach Real Estate Guide

Negotiating the Best Deal

Negotiation is a critical aspect of real estate transactions. Your agent can help you navigate the negotiation process to achieve the best possible outcome:

Offer Strategy:

- When buying a property, your agent can help you craft a competitive offer based on market conditions, comparable sales, and the seller's motivations.
- They will guide you on the best approach to contingencies, earnest money deposits, and closing timelines to strengthen your offer.

Counteroffers:

- If you receive a counteroffer, your agent will help you evaluate it and determine the best response. They can advise on adjusting terms such as price, contingencies, and closing dates to reach a mutually beneficial agreement.
- Effective negotiation requires balancing firmness with flexibility to achieve a successful deal.

Resolving Issues:

- During the inspection and appraisal phases, issues may arise that require renegotiation. Your agent will advocate on your behalf to address any concerns and negotiate repairs or price adjustments.

- They can also mediate disputes and ensure that both parties remain focused on reaching a successful closing.

Supporting You Through Closing

The closing process involves numerous steps and can be complex. Your agent will provide essential support to ensure a smooth and successful closing:

Coordinating Inspections and Appraisals:

- Your agent will coordinate with inspectors, appraisers, and other professionals to schedule necessary evaluations of the property. They will also help you interpret the results and determine any necessary actions.

- Ensuring these processes are completed efficiently and on time is crucial for meeting closing deadlines.

Reviewing Documents:

- Your agent will review all closing documents, including the closing disclosure, deed, and settlement statement, to ensure accuracy and completeness.
- They will explain the documents to you and address any questions or concerns you may have.

Final Walk-Through:

- Before closing, your agent will accompany you on a final walk-through of the property to ensure it is in the agreed-upon condition and any requested repairs have been completed.
- This step ensures that there are no surprises or issues before finalizing the purchase.

Closing Day:

- On closing day, your agent will be present to guide you through the process, ensuring all documents are signed, funds are transferred, and the keys are handed over.

- Their support and expertise help ensure a seamless transition and a successful completion of the transaction.

In conclusion, working with a knowledgeable and experienced real estate agent can greatly enhance your buying, selling, or investing experience in New Smyrna Beach. By choosing the right agent, communicating effectively, leveraging their resources, negotiating skillfully, and relying on their support through closing, you can achieve your real estate goals with confidence and success.

Chapter 13: Home Inspection and Appraisal Insights

Home inspections and appraisals are critical steps in the real estate transaction process. This chapter provides a comprehensive guide to understanding their importance, preparing for them, and navigating potential issues.

Importance of Home Inspections

A home inspection is a thorough examination of a property's condition, conducted by a professional inspector. It is essential for identifying any issues or defects that may affect the property's value or safety.

Buyer's Perspective:

- For buyers, a home inspection provides a detailed assessment of the property's condition, helping them make an informed decision and avoid unexpected expenses.
- The inspection report can be used to negotiate repairs or price adjustments with the seller.

Seller's Perspective:

- For sellers, a pre-listing inspection can identify potential issues that may arise during the buyer's inspection. Addressing these issues in advance can prevent delays and strengthen your position during negotiations.

- Providing a pre-listing inspection report can also build trust with potential buyers.

Preparing for a Home Inspection

Whether you are buying or selling, preparing for a home inspection involves several key steps:

Buyer Preparation:

- Choose a qualified home inspector with experience and good reviews. Your real estate agent can recommend reputable inspectors.
- Attend the inspection to ask questions and gain a better understanding of the property's condition. The

inspector will provide a detailed report outlining any issues found.

Seller Preparation:

- Ensure your property is accessible for the inspector, including the attic, basement, crawl spaces, and all rooms. Clear any obstacles that may hinder the inspection.
- Address any known issues beforehand, such as leaky faucets, faulty electrical outlets, or broken windows. This can improve the inspection results and reduce potential negotiation points.

Common Issues Found During Inspections

FLORIDA BEACH LIFE
New Smyrna Beach Real Estate Guide

Home inspections can reveal a variety of issues, ranging from minor repairs to major structural problems. Understanding common issues can help you prepare for potential outcomes:

Structural Issues:

- Inspectors often look for signs of structural problems, such as foundation cracks, uneven floors, and roof damage. These issues can be costly to repair and may affect the property's safety and value.

Plumbing and Electrical Systems:

- Plumbing issues, such as leaks, water pressure problems, and outdated pipes, are common findings.

Electrical issues, including outdated wiring, overloaded circuits, and faulty outlets, are also frequently identified.

HVAC Systems:

- Heating, ventilation, and air conditioning (HVAC) systems are inspected for proper operation, age, and maintenance. Issues such as inefficient heating or cooling, leaks, and outdated systems can impact the property's comfort and energy efficiency.

Roof and Exterior:

- The roof is examined for signs of damage, wear, and leaks. Exterior elements, such as siding, gutters, and windows, are also inspected for their condition and maintenance needs.

Interior and Appliances:

- Interior features, including walls, ceilings, floors, and built-in appliances, are inspected for damage and functionality. The inspector will check for signs of water damage, mold, and pest infestations.

Understanding Appraisals

An appraisal is an independent evaluation of a property's market value, conducted by a licensed appraiser. It is typically required by lenders to ensure the loan amount does not exceed the property's value.

FLORIDA BEACH LIFE
New Smyrna Beach Real Estate Guide

Purpose of Appraisal:

- The primary purpose of an appraisal is to protect the lender by ensuring the property's value supports the loan amount. It also provides buyers and sellers with an objective assessment of the property's worth.

Factors Affecting Appraisal:

- Appraisers consider various factors when determining a property's value, including its location, size, condition, and recent comparable sales (comps) in the area.

- Market trends, neighborhood amenities, and the overall condition of the property also influence the appraisal value.

Preparing for an Appraisal

Preparing for an appraisal involves several key steps to ensure the property is accurately valued:

Buyer Preparation:

- Provide the appraiser with relevant information about the property, including recent upgrades, improvements, and any unique features that may add value.

- Ensure the property is clean, well-maintained, and accessible for the appraiser's visit.

Seller Preparation:

- Compile a list of recent upgrades, renovations, and improvements to provide to the appraiser. Highlight any features that distinguish your property from others in the area.
- Address any minor repairs or maintenance issues before the appraisal to present the property in its best condition.

Navigating Potential Issues

FLORIDA BEACH LIFE
New Smyrna Beach Real Estate Guide

Both inspections and appraisals can uncover issues that need to be addressed. Navigating these issues effectively involves several key steps:

Inspection Issues:

- If the inspection reveals significant problems, buyers can negotiate with the seller for repairs, price reductions, or credits at closing. Be prepared to prioritize which issues are most important to address.
- Sellers should be open to reasonable repair requests and work with the buyer to reach a mutually agreeable solution.

Appraisal Issues:

- If the appraisal comes in lower than the agreed-upon purchase price, buyers and sellers may need to renegotiate the terms of the sale. Options include reducing the price, increasing the down payment, or challenging the appraisal with additional comps.
- Ensure all relevant information about the property is provided to the appraiser upfront to avoid potential undervaluation.

In conclusion, home inspections and appraisals are critical components of the real estate transaction process. By understanding their importance, preparing effectively, and navigating potential issues, you can ensure a smooth and successful transaction. Working with experienced professionals, including your real estate agent, inspector,

FLORIDA BEACH LIFE
New Smyrna Beach Real Estate Guide

and appraiser, will provide valuable insights and support throughout the process.

FLORIDA BEACH LIFE
New Smyrna Beach Real Estate Guide

Chapter 14: Closing the Deal: What to Expect

The closing process is the final step in the real estate transaction, where ownership of the property is transferred from the seller to the buyer. This chapter provides a comprehensive guide to understanding the closing process, preparing for closing

please continue

Please write in English language.

ChatGPT

Chapter 14: Closing the Deal: What to Expect (continued)

, and navigating the final steps to ensure a smooth and successful transaction.

Michael R. Linton, Author, Real Estate Broker eXp Realty
www.FloridaBeachLife.com

Understanding the Closing Process

The closing process involves several key steps and can take anywhere from a few days to several weeks, depending on the complexity of the transaction. It's essential to understand these steps to be well-prepared for closing day.

Final Walk-Through:

- Typically conducted a day or two before closing, the final walk-through allows the buyer to ensure that the property is in the agreed-upon condition and that any requested repairs have been completed.
- During the walk-through, check for any new issues or damage that may have occurred since the inspection. Verify that all included appliances and fixtures are present and functioning.

Reviewing Closing Documents:

- Both parties will need to review and sign several documents at closing. Key documents include the closing disclosure, deed, bill of sale, and loan documents.
- The closing disclosure outlines the final details of the mortgage loan, including the loan amount, interest rate, monthly payments, and closing costs. Review this document carefully and ensure all information is accurate.

Title Transfer:

- The title company will prepare the deed, which legally transfers ownership of the property from the seller to the buyer. Both parties will sign the deed, and it will be recorded with the local county recorder's office.
- Title insurance, which protects against future claims on the property, is typically purchased at this time. The buyer's lender usually requires this insurance.

FLORIDA BEACH LIFE
New Smyrna Beach Real Estate Guide

Preparing for Closing Day

Preparation is key to ensuring a smooth closing process. Here are several steps to take before closing day:

Gathering Necessary Documents:

- Buyers should bring a government-issued photo ID, proof of homeowner's insurance, and any required funds for closing costs and the down payment.
- Sellers should provide keys, garage door openers, and any necessary documentation, such as repair receipts or warranties.

Understanding Closing Costs:

- Closing costs typically range from 2% to 5% of the purchase price and can include fees for the loan origination, appraisal, title search, title insurance, escrow services, and recording the deed.

- Review the closing disclosure to understand the breakdown of these costs. Buyers should ensure they have the necessary funds available for these expenses.

Coordinating with Your Real Estate Agent and Lender:

- Stay in close communication with your real estate agent and lender leading up to closing day. They will provide guidance on any additional steps or documents needed.
- Confirm the closing date, time, and location, and ensure all parties involved are aware and prepared.

What Happens on Closing Day

Closing day is when all final documents are signed, funds are transferred, and ownership of the property is officially transferred to the buyer. Here's what to expect:

Signing Documents:

- Both the buyer and seller will sign several documents. The buyer will sign loan documents, including the promissory note and mortgage or deed of trust, committing to repay the loan.
- The seller will sign documents transferring ownership, such as the deed. Both parties may also sign additional documents, such as affidavits and disclosures.

Paying Closing Costs and Funding:

- The buyer will provide a cashier's check or wire transfer for the down payment and closing costs. The lender will transfer the loan funds to the escrow account.

- The title company or closing agent will disburse the funds to the appropriate parties, including paying off the seller's existing mortgage and any outstanding liens.

Recording the Deed:

- The title company or closing agent will record the deed with the county recorder's office, officially transferring ownership to the buyer. This step is crucial for the buyer to receive clear title to the property.
- Once recorded, the buyer will receive the keys and any necessary documents related to the property.

Post-Closing Steps

After closing, there are a few additional steps to take to ensure a smooth transition into your new home or the next phase of your property sale:

FLORIDA BEACH LIFE
New Smyrna Beach Real Estate Guide

Changing Utilities and Services:

- Buyers should transfer or set up utilities in their name, including electricity, water, gas, and internet services. Contact the utility companies a few days before closing to schedule the transfer.
- Sellers should cancel their services effective from the closing date to avoid any unnecessary charges.

Updating Your Address:

- Notify important parties of your new address, including the postal service, banks, credit card companies, insurance providers, and any subscription services.
- Update your address with the DMV and voter registration.

Maintaining Records:

- Keep copies of all closing documents, including the closing disclosure, deed, loan documents, and title insurance policy. These records are important for future reference and tax purposes.
- Store these documents in a safe place, such as a secure filing cabinet or a digital document storage service.

Celebrating Your New Home:

- Take time to celebrate your new home and the successful completion of the transaction. Moving can be stressful, so enjoy the moment and look forward to settling into your new space.

Addressing Any Post-Closing Issues:

- If any issues arise after closing, such as undisclosed property defects or title issues, contact your real estate agent or attorney for assistance. They can help navigate the process and resolve any problems.

In conclusion, the closing process is a critical step in the real estate transaction, requiring careful preparation, understanding of the necessary documents, and effective coordination with all parties involved. By following these steps and staying informed, you can ensure a smooth and successful closing, whether you are buying or selling a property in New Smyrna Beach.

Chapter 15: Future Trends and Market Predictions

The real estate market is dynamic and influenced by various factors, including economic conditions, demographic shifts, and technological advancements. This chapter provides insights into future trends and market predictions for New Smyrna Beach real estate to help you make informed decisions and stay ahead of the curve.

Economic Factors Influencing Real Estate

Economic conditions play a significant role in shaping the real estate market. Understanding these factors can help you anticipate market changes and make strategic decisions.

Interest Rates:

FLORIDA BEACH LIFE
New Smyrna Beach Real Estate Guide

- Interest rates impact mortgage affordability and buyer demand. Lower interest rates typically stimulate demand, while higher rates can slow down the market.
- Monitor interest rate trends and forecasts from the Federal Reserve and other financial institutions to anticipate their effects on the real estate market.

Employment and Income Levels:

- Employment rates and income levels influence buyers' purchasing power and confidence. Strong job growth and rising incomes can boost demand for housing.

- Keep an eye on local and national employment data to gauge market conditions and potential impacts on property values.

Inflation and Cost of Living:

- Inflation affects the cost of living and can influence buyer behavior. Higher inflation may lead to increased home prices and construction costs.
- Understand how inflation trends can impact your investment and adjust your strategies accordingly.

Demographic Shifts

FLORIDA BEACH LIFE
New Smyrna Beach Real Estate Guide

Demographic trends, such as population growth, age distribution, and household composition, influence housing demand and preferences.

Population Growth:

- New Smyrna Beach has experienced steady population growth, attracting retirees, families, and young professionals. This growth drives demand for various types of housing.
- Analyze population projections and migration patterns to identify emerging opportunities and areas of growth.

Aging Population:

FLORIDA BEACH LIFE
New Smyrna Beach Real Estate Guide

- The aging population trend continues to shape housing demand, with increased interest in age-restricted communities, single-story homes, and properties with accessibility features.
- Consider investing in properties that cater to the needs of older adults to capitalize on this demographic shift.

Millennial and Gen Z Buyers:

- Millennials and Gen Z are entering the housing market, bringing new preferences and priorities, such as sustainability, technology integration, and proximity to urban amenities.

- Stay informed about the preferences of younger buyers and adjust your investment or selling strategies to appeal to these demographics.

Technological Advancements

Technology is transforming the real estate industry, affecting how properties are marketed, sold, and managed.

Virtual Tours and Digital Marketing:

- Virtual tours, 3D walkthroughs, and drone photography have become essential tools for marketing properties, especially during the COVID-19 pandemic. These technologies enhance the buying experience and attract a wider audience.

- Invest in high-quality digital marketing to showcase your properties and reach potential buyers more effectively.

Smart Home Technology:

- Smart home features, such as automated lighting, security systems, and energy-efficient appliances, are increasingly popular among buyers. These technologies offer convenience, security, and cost savings.
- Consider incorporating smart home upgrades into your properties to increase their appeal and value.

Blockchain and Real Estate Transactions:

- Blockchain technology is revolutionizing real estate transactions by providing secure, transparent, and efficient processes for property transfers, title management, and smart contracts.
- Stay informed about developments in blockchain technology and its potential applications in real estate to streamline transactions and reduce fraud.

Environmental and Sustainability Trends

Sustainability and environmental considerations are becoming more important to buyers and investors.

Green Building Practices:

- Green building practices, such as using sustainable materials, energy-efficient designs, and water conservation measures, are gaining popularity. These practices can reduce environmental impact and operating costs.
- Explore opportunities to incorporate green building practices into your properties to attract eco-conscious buyers and increase long-term value.

Climate Change and Resilience:

- Climate change is influencing real estate markets, with increased focus on properties' resilience to natural disasters, such as hurricanes, flooding, and rising sea levels.

- Assess the climate risks in New Smyrna Beach and consider investing in properties with resilient features, such as elevated foundations and hurricane-proof construction.

Market Predictions for New Smyrna Beach

Based on current trends and projections, the New Smyrna Beach real estate market is expected to continue evolving in the coming years.

Continued Demand for Coastal Properties:

- New Smyrna Beach's appeal as a coastal destination will likely sustain strong demand for beachfront and waterfront properties. These properties are expected to appreciate in value due to their limited supply and high desirability.

- Monitor local development plans and zoning changes to stay ahead of emerging opportunities and potential challenges in the coastal property market.

Expansion of Mixed-Use Developments:

- Mixed-use developments that combine residential, commercial, and recreational spaces are becoming increasingly popular. These developments offer convenience and a sense of community, attracting a diverse range of buyers.

- Consider investing in or developing mixed-use properties to capitalize on this trend and meet the growing demand for integrated living environments.

Growth in Vacation Rentals and Tourism:

- The vacation rental market in New Smyrna Beach is expected to remain robust, driven by the city's tourism appeal. Properties that cater to short-term rentals, such as beachfront condos and homes with desirable amenities, will continue to be in high demand.
- Stay informed about local regulations and market trends to optimize your investment in vacation rental properties.

Rising Interest in Sustainable and Energy-Efficient Homes:

- As awareness of environmental issues grows, more buyers are seeking sustainable and energy-efficient homes. Properties with features such as solar panels, energy-efficient appliances, and green building materials will become increasingly attractive.
- Consider incorporating sustainability features into your properties to appeal to environmentally conscious buyers and enhance long-term value.

Technological Integration in Real Estate Transactions:

- The integration of technology in real estate transactions, such as digital signatures, blockchain, and virtual closings, will continue to streamline the buying and selling process. These advancements will make transactions more efficient and secure.

- Stay updated on technological advancements and adopt tools that can enhance your real estate transactions and improve the client experience.

Impact of Remote Work on Housing Preferences:

- The rise of remote work has shifted housing preferences, with more buyers seeking homes with dedicated office spaces, larger living areas, and proximity to outdoor recreational amenities. This trend is likely to persist, influencing demand in suburban and coastal areas.

FLORIDA BEACH LIFE
New Smyrna Beach Real Estate Guide

- Consider the needs of remote workers when marketing properties and highlight features that cater to a work-from-home lifestyle.

Potential Challenges and Considerations:

- While the market outlook is generally positive, potential challenges such as economic fluctuations, changes in interest rates, and regulatory shifts could impact the real estate market. Stay informed about broader economic trends and local policy changes to navigate these challenges effectively.
- Diversify your investment portfolio to mitigate risks and capitalize on different market segments.

Michael R. Linton, Author, Real Estate Broker eXp Realty
www.FloridaBeachLife.com

Strategies for Success in the Future Market

To succeed in the evolving New Smyrna Beach real estate market, adopt strategies that align with future trends and market predictions.

Stay Informed and Adaptable:

- Continuously monitor market trends, economic indicators, and demographic shifts to stay ahead of changes. Adapt your strategies to respond to emerging opportunities and challenges.
- Engage in ongoing education and professional development to enhance your knowledge and skills in the real estate industry.

FLORIDA BEACH LIFE
New Smyrna Beach Real Estate Guide

Leverage Technology and Innovation:

- Embrace technological advancements to streamline transactions, enhance marketing efforts, and improve property management. Utilize tools such as virtual tours, digital marketing platforms, and smart home technology.
- Stay open to innovative solutions that can improve efficiency and provide a competitive edge.

Focus on Sustainability and Resilience:

- Prioritize sustainability and resilience in your real estate investments. Consider the environmental

Michael R. Linton, Author, Real Estate Broker eXp Realty
www.FloridaBeachLife.com

impact of your properties and incorporate features that enhance energy efficiency and durability.
- Stay informed about climate risks and adopt practices that improve the resilience of your properties to natural disasters.

Build Strong Relationships:

- Cultivate strong relationships with clients, industry professionals, and the local community. Building trust and a positive reputation can lead to repeat business and valuable referrals.
- Engage in networking and collaboration to expand your reach and gain insights from other professionals in the industry.

Provide Exceptional Service:

- Deliver exceptional service to your clients by understanding their needs, providing personalized solutions, and maintaining clear communication throughout the transaction process.
- Focus on creating positive experiences that build long-term relationships and foster client loyalty.

In conclusion, the future of the New Smyrna Beach real estate market is shaped by various economic, demographic, and technological factors. By staying informed, embracing innovation, prioritizing sustainability, building strong relationships, and providing exceptional service, you can navigate the evolving market successfully and achieve your real estate goals. Whether you are buying, selling, or investing, these strategies will help you stay ahead of the curve and capitalize on the opportunities in this vibrant coastal community.

Final Thoughts

The "New Smyrna Beach Real Estate Guide" has provided you with comprehensive insights into the vibrant real estate market of this beautiful coastal city. From understanding the local market and finding your perfect home to navigating the buying and selling process and making informed investment decisions, this guide equips you with the knowledge and strategies needed for success.

As you move forward, remember that the real estate market is dynamic, and staying informed, adaptable, and client-focused will be key to your success. Whether you are a seasoned investor or a first-time homebuyer, the principles and strategies outlined in this guide will serve as valuable tools in your real estate journey.

Michael R. Linton, Author, Real Estate Broker eXp Realty
www.FloridaBeachLife.com

FLORIDA BEACH LIFE
New Smyrna Beach Real Estate Guide

Thank you for embarking on this journey with us, and we wish you the best of luck in your real estate endeavors in New Smyrna Beach.

Buy and Sell Your New Smyrna Beach Property with Michael Linton of eXp Realty

Introduction

Are you dreaming of owning a piece of paradise in New Smyrna Beach? Or maybe you're ready to sell your beachside property and embark on a new adventure? Whatever your real estate goals, Michael Linton of eXp Realty is here to make them a reality. With years of experience and a deep understanding of the local market, Michael is your go-to expert for all things real estate in New Smyrna Beach. Let's dive into how you can buy and sell your New Smyrna Beach real estate with Michael Linton of eXp Realty!

Why New Smyrna Beach?

FLORIDA BEACH LIFE
New Smyrna Beach Real Estate Guide

A Slice of Paradise

New Smyrna Beach, often dubbed the hidden gem of Florida, offers everything you could want in a coastal town. From its pristine beaches to its vibrant arts scene, there's something for everyone.

- Beautiful Beaches: Miles of sandy shores perfect for sunbathing, surfing, and shell collecting.
- Cultural Hub: Home to numerous art galleries, theaters, and music venues.
- Outdoor Activities: Boating, fishing, hiking, and more await adventure enthusiasts.

Thriving Community

Michael R. Linton, Author, Real Estate Broker eXp Realty
www.FloridaBeachLife.com

FLORIDA BEACH LIFE
New Smyrna Beach Real Estate Guide

The community spirit in New Smyrna Beach is contagious. Whether you're a long-time resident or a newcomer, you'll quickly feel at home.

- Friendly Locals: Warm and welcoming neighbors.
- Festivals and Events: From seafood festivals to art shows, there's always something happening.
- Great Schools: Quality education options for families with children.

The Buying Process with Michael Linton

Step-by-Step Guidance

Buying a home can be overwhelming, but with Michael Linton by your side, you'll have a smooth and enjoyable experience.

Michael R. Linton, Author, Real Estate Broker eXp Realty
www.FloridaBeachLife.com

FLORIDA BEACH LIFE
New Smyrna Beach Real Estate Guide

Initial Consultation

- Discuss your budget, preferences, and must-haves.
- Get pre-approved for a mortgage if necessary.

Home Search

- Michael will curate a list of properties that meet your criteria.
- Schedule viewings and tours at your convenience.

Making an Offer

- Michael will help you craft a competitive offer.
- Negotiate terms and conditions to get the best deal.

Closing the Deal

- Coordinate inspections, appraisals, and paperwork.
- Celebrate your new home once everything is finalized!

Michael R. Linton, Author, Real Estate Broker eXp Realty
www.FloridaBeachLife.com

Local Expertise

Michael Linton knows New Smyrna Beach like the back of his hand. His local knowledge is invaluable in finding the perfect home.

- Neighborhood Insights: Understand the pros and cons of different areas.
- Market Trends: Stay updated on the latest real estate trends and pricing.

Selling Your Home with Michael Linton

Preparing Your Home

First impressions matter! Michael will guide you through the steps to make your home market-ready.

Staging Tips

- Declutter and depersonalize your space.
- Consider minor repairs and updates.
- Enhance curb appeal with landscaping and fresh paint.

Professional Photography

High-quality photos are essential in attracting potential buyers. Michael ensures your property looks its best online and in marketing materials.

Effective Marketing

Michael utilizes a mix of traditional and digital marketing strategies to reach a broad audience.

- Online Listings: Your home will be listed on major real estate websites.
- Social Media: Targeted ads and posts to attract interested buyers.
- Open Houses: Organized events to showcase your property.

Negotiating Offers

With Michael's negotiation skills, you can rest assured you'll get the best possible price for your home.

- Review and compare offers.
- Negotiate terms that align with your goals.
- Ensure a smooth closing process.

FLORIDA BEACH LIFE
New Smyrna Beach Real Estate Guide

FAQs

How do I get started with buying or selling my New Smyrna Beach real estate?

Reach out to Michael Linton at eXp Realty for an initial consultation. He'll guide you through the entire process, whether you're buying or selling.

What makes New Smyrna Beach a great place to live?

From stunning beaches to a vibrant arts scene, New Smyrna Beach offers a high quality of life with a welcoming community.

How can I maximize the value of my home before selling?

Michael R. Linton, Author, Real Estate Broker eXp Realty
www.FloridaBeachLife.com

Michael will provide personalized advice on staging, minor repairs, and enhancements to boost your home's appeal and value.

What kind of support can I expect from Michael Linton during the buying process?

Michael offers comprehensive support, from finding the perfect home to closing the deal, ensuring a smooth and stress-free experience.

Conclusion

When it comes to buying and selling real estate in New Smyrna Beach, Michael Linton of eXp Realty is your trusted partner. His expertise, local knowledge, and commitment to client satisfaction make the process seamless and enjoyable. Whether you're looking to buy your dream home or sell your current property, Michael is here to help you every step of the way. Contact Michael Linton today and take the first step towards achieving your real estate goals in New Smyrna Beach!

Remember, buy and sell your New Smyrna Beach real estate with Michael Linton of eXp Realty to ensure a top-notch experience from start to finish.

FLORIDA BEACH LIFE
New Smyrna Beach Real Estate Guide

Michael R. Linton, Author, Real Estate Broker eXp Realty
www.FloridaBeachLife.com

www.ingramcontent.com/pod-product-compliance
Lightning Source LLC
Chambersburg PA
CBHW050205230526
45470CB00001B/243